Time And Gematria
IN DEUTERONOMY

Studies On The End of Days

Dr. Akiva Gamliel Belk
Dean of Jewish Studies
B'nei Noach Torah Institute, LLC

http://www.Jewishpath.org
http://www.bnti.us

For Information and
FREE Video Discussions etc.
on this book and other books please visit:

http://www.bnti.us/bjc16.html

Copyright © 2015	Publisher
Dr. Akiva Gamliel Belk	B'nai Noach Torah Institute, LLC,
Dr_Akiva_Gamliel@bnti.us	POst Office Box 14
	Cedar Hill, MiO 63016
All rights reserved	636-543-8000
ISBN - 13: 978-0692551370	
ISBN - 10: 0692551379	First Edition 2015

Table of Contents

Dedication..5
Introduction...7
Devarim Devarim..9
   Let's Connect The Letter Mem With Time............9
Devarim Ve'etchanan..25
   At That Time..25
Parshat Devarim Eikve...61
   Time Awareness...61
Parshat Devarim Re'ey...83
   Specific Direction of Time And Gematria............83
Parshat Devarim Shoftim..93
   The Time of First Fruits......................................93
Parshat Devarim Ki Teitzei...................................123
   Unique Mentions Of Time In The Torah............123
Parshat Devarim Ki Tavo.....................................137
   Time To Acknowledge We Are Blessed!...........137
Parshat Devarim Nitzavim....................................147
   The End of Days..147
Vayeilech..167
   Time of Rebellion at The End of Days..............167
Ha'azinu..175
   A Time of Justice And Security.........................175
     At The End of Days.......................................175
Devarim Vezot HaBrachah....................................189
   The Time of אֵשׁ דָּת The Fiery Torah 189
Scriptural Index..200
Gematria Index...207
About The Author..209
Books By Dr. Akiva Gamliel..................................211

Dedication

Oh Blessed One,
Almighty God Of All Creation,
Thank You for allowing me to write
and to publish this book on
Time and Gematria.

Mighty God of Israel,
Please bless each reader
with great Spiritual insight.

Blessed be Your Name
Forever and Ever!

Introduction

Dear Reader, studying, preparing and writing Time and Gematria has been a wonderful experience. I feel warm all over because of the deep Spiritual insights each Chapter delivers. It has been an enjoyable experience sharing points in time with Gematria.

I explain how we discover revelations hidden through The Holy Scriptures with Gematria at: http://www.bnti.us/bjc16.html

I have been afforded the unique opportunity on different ocassions throughout Time and Gematria to share my views on Bible prophecy and to share why Torah Observances are so important as we approach The End of Days.

Each Chapter is quite different from the others. All chapters have a common thread woven between Time and Gematria.

Please contact me with any questions or comments at: Dr_Akiva_Gamliel@bnti.us

Devarim Devarim
Deuteronomy 1.1 - 3.20

Chapter One

Let's Connect The Letter Mem With Time

Dear Ones, our goal in this discussion, is to help us make a connection with The Letter מ Mem. The Letter Mem has two forms. There is the normal Letter מ Mem and The Final Letter ם Mem.

Final Letters
The Final Letter ם Mem is One of Five Final Letters in Hebrew. The Final Letters are ך Chof, ם Mem, ן Nun, ף Pay, and ץ Tzaddi. When one of the Five Letters is the last Letter in a Hebrew Word, that Letter is ALWAYS written as a Final Letter.

The Hebrew Aleph Bet has twenty-two Letters and Five Final Letters. The Mem is a middle Letter of The Aleph Bet.

אבגדהוזחטיכל מ נסעפצקרשת

There are hidden mystical signs of revelation in The Hebrew Letters and Words of The Holy Scriptures. Hebrew is the original language. The Lord God used The Hebrew Language to Create everything. Hebrew is called Loshon Kodesh, i.e. The Holy Language. Each Hebrew Letter represents a number. Each Hebrew Letter is an אוֹת Oht, meaning 'A Sign'. The common term is Gematria. The definition for Gematria is 'A Kabbalistic Spiritual Method of interpreting The Hebrew Scriptures by computing the numerical value of Hebrew Words in The Holy Scriptures, based on those of their constituent letters.' The Gematria Sign of The Letter Mem is 40. The Gematria Sign for The Final Mem is 600.

The Final Letter ם Mem and The Letter ס Samech are the only Two Hebrew Letters that makes a complete 360-degree circle. The Final Letter Mem was suspended in air without touching or connecting on any side to the Two Tablets of stone when The Lord God Wrote The Ten Commandments on Mount Sinai. The Lord Made The Final Mem stand in place without falling. The Letter Mem is an eternal Letter. The Mem does not have a beginning or end. In addition to the Words we are going to study, The Words מֹשֶׁה Moses and מָשִׁיחַ Moshiach / Messiah each begin with The Letter Mem.

God Willing, our goal is to discover how Time, Hebrew Letters, Hebrew Words and Hebrew Gematria connect and relate in The Book of Deuteronomy to Moses our Teacher and The People of Israel. We will observe the wisdom in Time. It is written. We will observe, perhaps one or two picture frames in the movie of Time. King Solomon wrote, 'To everything there is a season and time to every purpose under the heavens,' Ecclesiastics 3.1. In each Chapter of Time and Gematria will examine specific points in Time that are woven together with Gematria. Together, Time and Gematria will open doors of hidden revelations.

Deuteronomy 1.1 - 3
These are The Words which Moses shared with all Israel on this side of the Jordan in the

wilderness, in the Arabah opposite the Red Sea, between Paran, and Tophel, and Laban, and Hazeroth, and Dizahab. There is *Eleven Days' journey from Horeb by the way of Mount Seir to Kadesh-Barnea. And it happened in Year Forty, in Month Eleven, on Day One to The Month that Moses shared with The people of Israel, about every Command that The Lord Said to him with them.*

The Eleven Day Journey Mystically points to the Times when The People of Israel spoke slander. דִּבָּה Dee Bawh meaning slander.

דִּבָּה
Dee Bawh / To Slander
11 = 5 ה 2 ב 4 ד

Unfortunately, during the forty Years in The Wilderness slander and defamation was part of the journey of The People of Israel. However, there is another Eleven. The Second Eleven is a measurement of Time, i.e., *'in Year Forty, and in Month Eleven'*. The Second Eleven Mystically points to good because the sins of

The People of Israel in The Wilderness were forgiven. The People of Israel repented for past failings. The offenders had died in The Wilderness. טָב Tawv means 'Good.'

טָב
Tawv / Good
11 = 2 ב 9 ט

The People of Israel left Egypt in the year 2448 FC in Month One in Day Fifteen. That was a long time ago. The Torah Says it was Forty Years. We already know the number Forty relates to The Letter Mem. We know The Letter Mem represents a circle. The people of Israel were returning to entering The Holy Land of Cannan. They had gone full circle so to speak. See Joshua 4.19 and Joshua 5.10 - 11.

There were 30 days left in Month Eleven and 29 Days left in Month Twelve. They were 59 days from completing Year Forty. חוֹמָה Choh Maw means wall. חוֹמָה Choh Mawh, meaning 'A wall' surrounded the city of Jerico. הַחוֹמָה Hah Choh Mawh meaning 'The Wall' fell,

Joshua 6.20.

חוֹמָה
Choh Maw / Wall
ח 8 ו 6 מ 40 ה 5 = 59

Moses was 37 Days away from turning 120 years of age. Moses would die in 37 Days on his Birthday. Our Sages Teach that Moses was in Mitzraim / Egypt 40 years, In Midian 40 years and the Midbar / Wilderness 40 Years. Each Word begins with The Letter מ Mem.

Mitzraim / Egypt
מִצְרַיִם
מ 40 צ 90 ר 200 י 10 ם נ 40 = 380

Midian
מִדְיָן
מ 40 ד 4 י 10 ן 50 = 104

Wilderness
מִדְבָּר
מ 40 ד 4 ב 2 ר 200 = 246

Our Sages Teach that Moses spent 40 Years in Mitzraim, 40 Years in Midian and 40 Years in Midbar. 120 = 40 + 40 + 40

Moses dies on his day of birth at 120 Years of age, Deuteronomy 34.7.

The 2016 Bible Journeys Calendar readers will observe that Moses simultaneous fasted for Three Forty Day and Night periods. Moses fasted from the Day he received The Torah, The Commandments and The Covenant to Yom Kipper, which is The Day of Atoning.

Moses fasted three forty day periods one after the other plus the day before and the in between days, a total of 122 to 123 days. The Seventh of Sivan is not counted. This is the Day Moses climbed Mt Sinai to receive The Commandments. The Day Moses prepares the second set of Tablets was 29th of Av. This Day was not included in the fast days. So how can 122 days be 123 days? The question is, did Moses Fast on 6 Sivan, the preparation Day? Our Sages Teach Moses was very busy helping

The People prepare to receive The Torah. Did Moses eat a Sabbath meal that night? It is not likely given Moses understanding of purity. It is likely that Moses fasted to be in a state of readiness to receive The Torah. Why is this such an important question?

Numbers 33.39
And Aaron was a hundred and twenty-three years old when he died in Mount Hor.

One-Hundred-Twenty-Three Days ties Aharon, The High Priest to Shavuot and Yom Kippur. In other Words The High Priest that makes atonement is a bridge spanning between receiving The Torah to The Day he seeks forgiveness for The People of Israel.

Fast One
Exodus 24.16 - Fast one from Sivan 7 to 17 Tammuz. The 17th of Tammuz is when the Roman soldiers breached the Holy City in their conquest to destroy our Second Holy Temple in 3830 FC. Rabbi Nachman Zakon, The Jewish Experience 2,000 Years Shaar Press

(Brooklyn, New York: Mesorah Publications, Ltd. 2003), p 11

Exodus 32.15 - 19
And Moses turned, and went down from the mount, and the two tablets of The Testimony were in his hand. The Tablets were written on both their sides; on the one side, and the other were they written. And The Tablets were the work of God, and the writing was the writing of God, engraved upon The Tablets. And when Joshua heard the noise of The People as they shouted, he said to Moses, 'There is a sound like a war in the camp.' And He / Moses Said, 'It is not the voice of those who shout for mastery. Nor is it the voice of those who cry for being overcome; but the sound of those who sing do I hear.' And it came to pass, as soon as He came near to the camp, that He Saw the calf, and the dancing; and Moses' anger burned hot, and he threw The Tablets from his hands and broke them beneath the mount.

Fast Two
Exodus 32.29 - 35
For Moses had said, Consecrate yourselves

today to The Lord, every man against his son, and against his brother; that he may bestow upon you a blessing this Day. And it came to pass on the next Day, that Moses said to the people, You have sinned a great sin, and now I will go up to The Lord; perhaps I shall make an atonement for your sin. And Moses returned to The Lord and Said, 'Oh, this people have sinned a great sin, and have made them gods of gold. Now, if you will forgive their sin; and if not, blot me, I beg you, from your book that you have written.' And The Lord Said to Moses, 'Whoever has sinned against Me, him will I blot from My Book. Therefore now go, lead the people to the place about which I have spoken to you; behold, my Angel shall go before you; nevertheless in The Day when I Punish I Will Punish their sin upon them.' And the Lord Plagued the people because they made the calf, which Aaron made.

How do we know this second fast was for 40 Days? Deuteronomy 9. 12 - 18

In Verse Twelve Moses received The Tablets

when The Lord Informed him of The People's sin. Then he went down to them. Then he broke the Tablets. Then the next Day He returns to pray on Mt Sinai. Notice what The Torah Says.

Deuteronomy 9.11 - 12
And it came to pass at the end of Forty Days and Forty Nights, that The Lord Gave me The Two Tablets of Stone, The Tablets of The Covenant. And The Lord Said to me, 'Arise, get down quickly from here; for your people, which you have brought out of Egypt, have corrupted themselves. They have quickly turned aside from the way that I Commanded them. They have made themselves a molten image.'

How do we know Moses second Fast followed the first? How do we know the second Fast was also for Forty Days and Nights?

Deuteronomy 9.15 - 19
So I turned and came down from The Mount, and The Mount Burned with fire, and The Two

Tablets of the covenant were in my two hands. And I looked, and, behold, you had sinned against The Lord your God, and had made yourselves a molten calf; you had turned aside quickly from the way that the Lord Had Commanded you. And I took The Two Tablets, and threw them out of my two hands, and broke them before your eyes. And I fell down before The Lord, as at the First, Forty Days and Forty Nights; I did not eat bread, nor drink water, because of all your sins that you sinned, in doing wickedly in the sight of The Lord, to provoke Him to anger. For I was afraid of the anger and hot displeasure, with which The Lord was angry with you to destroy you. But The Lord listened to me at that time also.

Fast Three:
Deuteronomy 10.10 - 11
And I stayed in the mount, according to the First Time, Forty days and Forty Nights; and The Lord listened to me at that time also, and The Lord would not destroy you. And The Lord Said to me, 'Arise, go on your journey before

the people, that they may go in and possess the land, which I swore to their fathers to give to them.'

120 Days and Nights = 40 Days and Nights + 40 Days and Night + 40 Days and Nights

Within the Community of The People of Israel, there are some who pray each day each morning, afternoon and night. Some also pray at the mid of Night. The morning prayers maybe thirty minutes or longer on average. Afternoon prayers are perhaps fifteen minutes. Evening prayers are about twenty minutes. These are on normal Days. The Elul, Month, leading up to Rosh HaShannah, prayer time increases significantly. Then on Rosh HaShannah morning prayers may last from eight AM to three in the afternoon. On Yom Kippur, we fast from one night to the next night that is about twenty-six hours. On Erev Yom Kippur at Kol Nidre about three hours. On Yom Kippur, we pray from early morning to night. It is understandable that one might be a little weary.

What about Moses. He did not just fast One Day and Night. Moses fasted for about 123 Days and Nights. Moses bowed down, prayed and interceded for The People of Israel during the middle Forty Days and Nights. The greatness of Moses is a challenging connection for us. I can relate to a tiny portion of what Moses experienced. What about you?

When we say 'In the Wilderness' the Word is Bamidbar.

בַּמִּדְבָּר
248 = 200 ר 2 ב 4 ד 40 מ 2 ב

The positive Observances of Ha Torah are 248. The organs in our body are 248. We see a relationship between the being in the wilderness, the positive Commands of The Torah and the organs of our body.

Devarim 1.3 is informing us that the wilderness experience is coming to an end in 59 days. Moses Leadership and hands on Teaching is coming to an end in 37 Days. The Lord Has

Moses revisit the Observances with The People of Israel. Think of how that felt for Moses. He would die. He would not enter the Land with his people. The people who were taught Ha Torah at Moses' feet were already feeling the loss of their Great Teacher.

Devarim Ve'etchanan
Deuteronomy 3.23 - 7.11

Chapter Two

At That Time

Chapter One shared easier to see Gematrias related to Time. Lesson Two requires us to seek. Individuals who seek and seek for answers want to know. They don't give up. They are persistent. As it happens, the Time and Gematria that we are discussing in Parshat Ve'etchanan requires us to be diligent in our discovery. It will be enjoyable when we get there.

The Word עֵת Ayt means 'Time.' בָּעֵת Baw Ayt means In Time, On Time, At A Time, Through Time, and With Time'. We are going to consider Deuteronomy 3.23. The best translation for Verse 23 is '*At That Time.*' We will go with this translation. The Word עֵת Ayt occurs 73 times and בָּעֵת Baw Ayt occurs 90 times in The Hebrew Scriptures. The difference between עֵת Ayt and בָּעֵת Baw Ayt is The Letter ב Bet. The ב Bet makes The Word עֵת Ayt 'A Point In Time.' We classify בָּעֵת Baw Ayt as a definite place in time. When Moses Says בָּעֵת Baw Ayt, he is making reference to a specific place in Time. Our goal is to try and determine what that place in time is. We will first view The verse then we will determine The Year.

Devarim 3.23

וָאֶתְחַנַּן אֶל־יְהוָה בָּעֵת הַהִוא לֵאמֹר:

Deuteronomy 3.23
And I pleaded with The Lord **at that time**, *saying,*

What was 'At that Time'? What is Moses referencing? The People of Israel knew. The Torah does not note anyone questioning Moses. No one asked Moses, 'What time are you talking about?'

Moses spoke these Words thousands of years ago. What was apparent then may not be apparent now. Does anyone know of which

Time Moses was speaking?

We begin our discovery with the Seventh Day of Miriam's affliction for speaking evil against Moses. Miriam spoke Loshon Hara against Moses. The Lord Called her out in front of all The People of Israel and rebuked her. Miriam was removed from the camp. Miriam was required to live outside the camp. Miriam was separated from The People of Israel for Seven Days. We begin our discovery on the Seventh Day of Miriam's separation. Miriam was allowed to return to the camp. It was on that Day Moses sent the 12 spies into the Land of Canaan. These events are easier to follow when one uses The 2016 Bible Journeys Calendar.

29 Sivan 2449 FC
The spies left the encampment at Paran one year and 74 Days after being delivered from Egypt by The Lord. It is necessary for me to make a distinction. If one studies The 2016 Bible Journeys Calendar, they will Observe several important Time points. In the first year, 2448 FC [From Creation] on this specific Day

Moses was in Day Twenty-Two of receiving the first set of Tablets on Mt. Sinai. Our point in Time is the following year. We are One Year and 74 Days away from the anniversary of the Day The People of Israel Killed the Passover Lamb, i.e. 29 Sivan 2449 FC. [16 Days in Nissan + 29 Days in Iyar + 29 Days in Sivan = 74 Days]

In Chapter One, we discovered that Moses fasted for three periods of Forty Days and Forty Nights in a row. When one fasts, they afflict their body. During the Time of fasting Moses removed himself from all forms of pleasure. Moses did not eat or drink. Moses did not have a physical relationship with his wife. During the Times of fasting Moses led a life of austerity. Moses maintained a life of physical purity so he could receive The Ten Commandments and intercede for The People of Israel when they sinned. After the Three periods of fasting, i.e. Yom Kippur Moses experienced a Supernatural Revelation of which he did not share with anyone. Only The Lord God knew. Moses realized he must be prepared to appear before The Lord God on a seconds notice. So Moses separated from strong drink and physical relationships with his wife. Moses gave up everything that might cause him to be physically impure.

Moses stopped having physical relations with his wife. When a husband and wife have physical relations, each become impure until nightfall. After nightfall, each must visit the Mikvah to immerse himself / herself entirely in water before they return to physical purity. The Mikvah for men and women is separate. When one is impure, they may not touch The Torah!

Later, Miriam learns that Moses separated from his wife, Zipporah. Rabbi Avrohom Davis, The Mesudah Chumash A New Linear Translation Bamidbar (Hoboken New Jersey, KTVA Publishing House, Inc., 1995) p 157

After Miriam learned that Moses separated from Zipporah, she simply shared, i.e. spread the news to Aharon. Even though what Miriam shared was accurate and entirely true it is

Loshon Harah. Miriam spread gossip. Gossip. Miriam slandered Moses. Numbers Twelve shares the story.

When The Torah Says The Lord Suddenly called to Moses, Aharon, and Miriam in Numbers 12.4 only Moses came out immediately. Miriam was in a state of impurity do to marital relations. Aharon was also in a state of impurity do to marital relations. It was then they realized why Moses separated from his wife. Moses needed to remain in a state purity because The Divine Presence constantly revealed Prophesy to him. The Lord God revealed Moses' superiority. Miriam was punished because she shared gossip / slander with Aharon.

Numbers 12.11

וַיֹּאמֶר אַהֲרֹן אֶל־מֹשֶׁה בִּי אֲדֹנִי אַל־נָא תָשֵׁת עָלֵינוּ חַטָּאת אֲשֶׁר נוֹאַלְנוּ וַאֲשֶׁר חָטָאנוּ׃

חָטָאנוּ
Chaw Taw Noo / Our Sin
ח 8 ט 9 א 1 נ 50 ו 6 = 74

Aharon pleaded, 'Oh, my lord, I beg you, lay not the sin upon us, because we have done foolishly, and because חָטָאנוּ meaning 'we have sinned.' We count 74 Days from The Day The Lord God Delivered B'nei Israel's from slavery.

We begin our discovery with the Day Miriam returned to the Camp of The People of Israel. For Seven Days all The People of Israel were reminded of Miriam's sin. It was with this reminder that the spies were sent forth for Forty Days. Are we beginning to see the cycle of Forty, i.e. The Letter Mem?

It may seem trivial to us regarding Miriam's sin of simply sharing Moses was no longer having a physical relationship with his wife. Notice how The Lord God reacted to Miriam's comment to Aharon. The Lord God rebuked Miriam in front of all Israel. Miriam became leprous. Miriam was separated from the encampment of the people she loved for Seven Days. The Lord God Asks Miriam, *'Why are you not afraid to speak against My Servant, Moses?'* Numbers 12.8 Moses pleads with The

Lord God. The Lord God Says to Moses, *'If her father were to spit in her face would she not be in shame for Seven Days?'* Numbers 12.14 - Miriam was a Prophetess. Miriam was highly respected. Miriam was in a position of great authority. It is CLEAR that The Lord God is Teaching Miriam, Aaron and The People of Israel an important lesson. The Lord God Desires that we know the seriousness of the Words we choose to use. We need to take this Teaching seriously!! The Gematria for לְמַד Lee Mahd meaning To Teach is 74. The Gematria for דַע Dah meaning to know is also 74.

לְמַד
Lee Mahd / To Teach
74 = 4 ד 40 מ 30 ל

דַע
Dah / To Know
74 = 70 ע 4 ד

Numbers 13.1 - 3
And The Lord Spoke to Moses, Saying, 'Send

for yourself men, and have them scout everything from Aleph to Tav of the land of Canaan, which I am Giving to The People of Israel; Send them, one great man from each of his father's tribes. Each must be a leader among them. And Moses sent them from the desert of Paran on The Word of The Lord. All were men of distinction; They were chiefs of the People of Israel.'

Those who study with me know that I often include The Words 'Everything from Aleph to Tav' when the Word אֶת Eht is used. The Word אֶת eht occurs thousands of times in The Holy Scripture for a reason. Many times the reason is to inform us of the inclusiveness of what is being said. The point is; nothing is left out. Everything is included. Chagigah 12b 1 - The Bahir (Row man & Littlefield Publishers, Inc. Lanham, Maryland 1995) pp. 108,109

Every Tribe sent a representative except for the Tribe of Levi. Numbers 13.4-16 lists the leaders from each Tribe. The Levites believed The Word of The Lord. They did not need to spy on The Land of Cannan.

09 Av 2449
The Spies return after Forty Days of spying out The Land of Canaan.

Ten of the twelve spies presented an evil report to B'nei Yisroel. Then B'nei Yisroel rebelled against The Lord. Due to our parents rebellion The People of Israel were not permitted to enter the Promised Land.

Numbers 13.26 - 27
And they returned from searching The Land after Forty Days. And they came to Moses, and to Aaron, and to all the congregation of B'nei Yisroel, to the wilderness of Paran, to Kadesh; and brought back word to them, and to all the congregation, and showed them the fruit of the land. And they told him and said, We came to The Land where you sent us, and surely it flows with milk and honey, and this is its fruit.

Numbers 13.28 - 29
However, the people, who inhabit the land, are

strong, and the cities are very greatly fortified [with walls] and moreover we saw the children of Anak there. The Amalekites dwell in the southern part of the land; and the Hittites, and the Jebusites, and the Amorites, dwell in the mountains; and the Canaanites dwell by the sea, and by the side of the Jordan.

Ten leaders expressed serious concerns about the people who dwelt in the land. They said, *'The land truly flows with milk and honey.'* Look at the magnificent fruit. However, there are some very scary people who occupy the land.

Numbers 13.30
And Caleb silenced everything from Aleph to Tav of The People and confidently said to Moses, 'We can go up and consume them. For we more than measure up, we are capable of doing it!'

Caleb was General of the Army of Yisroel. He assured The People of Israel that they were more than capable of defeating the enemy.

Then the spies representing Ten of Yisroel's Tribes chimed in. They had a different opinion. How qualified was their opinion? Were they battle tested like Joshua?

Numbers 13. 31 - 33
But the men who went up with him said, 'We are not able to go up against the people; for they are stronger than us.' And, they spread slander about The Land they spied for B'nei Israel, saying, 'The land, through which we have gone to spy, is A Land that consumes its inhabitants; and all the people that we saw in it are men of a great stature. And there we saw everything from Aleph to Tav of the Giants, the sons of Anak, who came from the Nephilim; and we were like as grasshoppers in their sight, and so were we in their sight.'

In our age, we have terms that describe different mental conditions. What do you think? Is it possible that all of The People of Israel had PTSD Post Traumatic Stress Disorder resulting from their slavery and brutal treatment in Egypt? B'nai Yisroel went through many hardships due to being captive. Do you think they may have had Stockholm Syndrome? Were they brainwashed by their captors? What type of individual, family, group and community issues were each dealing with? We can only imagine.

I ask these questions because of how quickly B'nei Yisroel turned away from The Lord. From time to time, it seems like B'nei Israel snaps instead of doing what they should.

We notice that there is a difference of opinion between Joshua, Caleb, and the other spies. Having differences of opinion among B'nei Yisroel is not unusual. It's what we do with our opinions that makes the difference. The Ten spies predetermined that B'nei Yisroel was 'not able to go up against the people'. In their opinion, the inhabitants were stronger than B'nei Yisroel. The spies described how small they were in comparison to the giants who were descendants of the fallen / the sons of Anak. The Ten spies compared themselves to grasshoppers next to the giants. They frightened B'nei Yisroel.

The Ten spies spread slander against the Promised Land. וַיֹּצִיאוּ דִּבַּת הָאָרֶץ 'They brought forth a report on The Land.' They said, 'The Land consumes its inhabitants.' This was a lie and part of their evil report. Our Sages Teach they witnessed many funerals while spying out the Land. There were so many people dying that the spies went unnoticed. This was Divine Providence working in their behalf, but instead of taking this point of view, Ten of the Leaders interpreted this as The Land that consumed its inhabitants. They spoke evil about the land. Rabbi Nosson Scherman, The Stone Edition The Chumash (Mesorah Publications, Ltd., Brooklyn, N.Y. 1993), p 803

The Ten spies were respected leaders among B'nei Yisroel, who agreed to speak evil regarding The Land of Canaan. What they did was wrong, yet this shows us the impact ten important leaders had on The People of Israel. When we, B'nei Yisroel, unite, we can do amazing things!

B'nei Yisroel rebelled based on the report of Ten well-respected spies.

When we speak of the Words, '*At That Time*,' could it be a point of reference to The Time B'nei Israel united for the wrong reasons?

Bamidbar 14.1
וַתִּשָּׂא כָּל־הָעֵדָה וַיִּתְּנוּ אֶת־קוֹלָם וַיִּבְכּוּ הָעָם בַּלַּיְלָה הַהוּא:

Numbers 14.1
[ת – SIGN] *And the entire community [except The Tribe of Levi] lifted up everything from Aleph to Tav of their voice and cried and wept through the night.*

בָּעֵת
Baw Ayt / At That Time
ב 2 ע 70 ת 400 = 472

בְּכִיתָם
Bih Cee Tehm / They weep
ב 2 כ 20 י 10 ת 400 ם 40 = 472

We Observe the Mystical connection to '*At That Time*' as 'Weeping'. Is this what Moses was making reference to when he wrote '*At That Time'?* It is a piece of the picture as we shall see.

I cannot emphasize how significant the Words of Verse One are. First the Verse begins with וַתִּשָּׂא Vah - Tee Shaw meaning 'And to lift up' Normally The Letter ת Tav is not part of this Word.

In the past, I have written about paying close attention to The Letter ת Tav. The Letter ת Tav is a Mystical Letter. When The Letter ת Tav appears as it does here, The ת Tav is a Sign to pay attention. We should seek for additional meaning. Normally the first Word in Verse One would be נָשָׂא Naw Saw, meaning '*to Lift up*'. However, The Word is וַתִּשָּׂא Vah - Tee Shaw. The Letter נ Nun is replaced by The Letter ת Tav. We must determine what the purpose is for replacing The Letter נ with The Letter ת Tav. Could it be that this is what Moses was making reference to when he said,

'At That Time'? Was The Letter ת Tav what Moses was referring to?

The root Word for וַתִּשָּׂא Vah - Tee Shaw has different meanings. Here we need to pay attention to the other meanings as well. Each Word uses the same Letters. The spelling is exactly the same. The only difference is with the Vowels. נִשָּׂא Nee Saw means 'to be misled or to be deceived'. Lets review.

<u>First</u>, וַתִּשָּׂא Vah - Tee Shaw meaning *'And to lift up.'*
<u>Second</u>, The Root Word is נָשָׂא Naw Saw, meaning *'to Lift up.'*
<u>Third</u>, The Letter נ Nun in נָשָׂא Naw Saw was replaced by The Letter ת Tav. [תִּשָּׂא] The Letter ו Vav of וַתִּשָּׂא Vah - Tee Shaw is a connecting Letter that means *'and'.*
<u>Fourth</u>, The Letter The ת Tav is a Sign to pay attention and to look for additional meaning.

Notice the meaning in the Two Words following וַתִּשָּׂא Vah - Tee Shaw. כָּל־הָעֵדָה Cawl - Haw Ay Dawh means *'All the community'* or

'All the witnesses'. All the Community includes members of The Sanhedrin and The Seventy Elders. The Sanhedrin was the Jewish Judges of The High Court. They were convinced that Moses and Aaron misled them. Rabbi Nosson Scherman, The Stone Edition The Chumash (Mesorah Publications, Ltd., Brooklyn, N.Y. 1993), p. 803 All The Judges and The Seventy Elders of B'nei Yisroel raised their voices and shouted. Rabbi Menachem M. Scheerson, Torah Chumash Shemot Kehot Publication Society (Brooklyn, NY 2006) p 86 B'nei Yisroel followed the lead of the High Court. They cried and wept through the night just as their leaders did.

Numbers 14.2
They murmured against Moses and Aaron; All of B'nei Yisroel [except The Tribe of Levi] and all of the Community [except The Tribe of Levi] *said to them, 'Would to God that we had died in the land of Egypt! Would to God we had died in this wilderness!'*

We need to take a minute to exeronate The

Tribe of Levi, who consistently took the high ground when B'nei Yisroel had issues. The Levites did not sin with the golden calf. Nor did they sin with B'nei Yisroel in the matter of the spies evil report. Rabbi Moshe Weissman, The Midrash Says Bamidbar (Brooklyn, New York: Benei Yakov Publications 1980), pp 157; 180, Rabbi Dr. H. Freedman, Midrash Rabba Babmidbar (New York, NY: The Soncino Press 1983) - Midrash Rabbah p 72 [br 3.5] - Rabbi Menachem M. Scheerson, Torah Chumash Shemot Kehot Publication Socierty (Brooklyn, NY 2006) p 253

The Midrash Says, The Sanhedrin complained to Moses saying, 'We accept the decree of death, but should we die at the hand of these idolaters in Eretz Canaan? It would have been better to have died in Egypt or to have passed away here in the wilderness.' Rabbi Moshe Weissman, The Midrash Says Bamidbar (Brooklyn, New York: Benei Yakov Publications 1980), p 170 How did The Lord Respond? 'It shall be as you wish'. How was The Word of The Lord fulfilled? Every Erev

Tish B'Av Moses would say to the men of war, those who rebelled against The Lord and those who were decreed to die during these Forty Years 'Dig A grave for yourself.' Each man dug a grave for himself and rested that night in the grave. Those who reached the age of sixty would pass away during the night of weeping. This was about 15,000 every year. 570,000 of the 600,000 men who were between 20 to 60 passed away like this each year. Rabbi Moshe Weissman, The Midrash Says Bamidbar (Brooklyn, New York: Benei Yakov Publications 1980), p 170

Can we imagine what it was like for the wives, children, relatives, and friends of those decreed to die in The Wilderness each year as the night of weeping approached? What was it like for The Judges, and The Sanhedrin who spoke the Words 'let us die here in The Wilderness?' What was it like for them knowing these men were dying because of their unjust faithfulness ruling? What was it like, in the month of Av, for B'nei Yisroel when the 9th of Av approached each year? What did it feel like watching thousands upon thousands of graves being dug? How did this impact The People of Israel? We have already discussed the Mystical connection of '*At That Time*' to weeping on the eve of the 9th of Av. How did the community of Yisroel feel knowing it was their Judges that spoke the words '*Let us die in The Wilderness*'? We should ask ourselves, how would I feel if I were one of the men between Twenty to Sixty that refused to fight for the Holy Land and who rebelled? What if I were one of the men that mummered and complained against the Lord? What if I were one of the men that said I wanted to return to Egypt, i.e. the idolatrous practices of Egypt. The ladies did not die because they remained faithful to The Lord quietly within their tents. Rabbi Moshe Weissman, The Midrash Says Bamidbar (Brooklyn, New York: Benei Yakov Publications 1980), p 180 The Sanhedrin and The Seventy Elders lead the Community in this very emotionally charged rebellion against Moses and Aaron. They exclaimed:

Numbers 14.3
And why has The Lord brought us to This

Land, to fall by the sword so that our wives and our children should become prey? Would it not be better for us to return into Egypt?

Up until this point according to our Sages The Sanhedrin and The Seventy Elders participated in the rebellion.

Numbers 14.1

- כָּל־הָעֵדָה Cawl - Haw Ay Daw meaning *All the Community / Congregation or All the Witnesses.* The Sanhedrin and The Seventy Elders are included.

Numbers 14.2

- כֹּל בְּנֵי יִשְׂרָאֵל Kol - B'nei Yisroel meaning *All of The People of Israel*

כָּל־הָעֵדָה Kawl - Haw Ay Daw meaning. *All the Community / Congregation*

Numbers 14.4
And the men said one to another, 'Let us appoint a chief and let us return to Egypt.'

Numbers 14.10

וַיֹּאמְרוּ כָּל־הָעֵדָה לִרְגּוֹם אֹתָם - *And The Entire Congregation Said 'Stone Them'*, refering to Joshua and Caleb.

Who has the authority to make such a decision? Who has the authority to appoint a leader over B'nei Yisroel? Who has the authority to sit in judgment?

It is very important for us to remember that The Lord Requires faithfulness from His People. We depend on our Leadership to help us stay on the right course. What happened here? In Deuteronomy 1.32 Moses said that **_'at that time'_** The People did not Trust The Lord their God. Why did our relatives of Years past fail to trust The Lord after all the Miracles He preformed? Why was B'nei Yisroel so willing to turn away from The Lord? We continue to read the extent of how distant B'nei Yisroel were willing to go in their rebellion to The Lord.

Numbers 14.5 - 6
Then Moses and Aaron fell on their faces

before all the assembly of the congregation of The People of Israel. And Joshua the son of Nun, and Caleb the son of Jephunneh, which were of those who spied the land, tore their clothes;

We see ONLY four men speaking up for The Lord and The Land of Canaan. The Sanhedrin and the Seventy Elders did not step up. They did not join them. Was this the Time Moses was speaking of when he said 'At That Time?

Numbers 14.7 - 9
And they spoke to all the Congregation of The People of Israel, saying, 'The land, which we passed through to spy, is a very good land. If the Lord Desires us to have it, then He Will Bring us into this Land, and Give it to us; a Land that flows with milk and honey. However, do not rebel against The Lord and do not fear the people of The Land; for they are like bread for us; their protection is removed from them, and The Lord is with us; do not be afraid of them.

Numbers 14.10
The entire community said that they should be stoned to death, [but just then] The Glory of The Lord Appeared in The Tent of Meeting before all The People of Israel.

Not any man has the authority to pass judgment on his fellow man. Who has the authority to judge? Who has the authority to pass judgment on stoning a guilty individual? Again we see The Sanhedrin's involvement in this rebellion.

The Sanhedrin felt like Moses and Aharon had deceived them. They felt like Moses and Aharon had misled them. I have already shown that The Root Word for וַתִּשָּׂא Vah - Tee Shaw has different meanings. We know that The Root Word for וַתִּשָּׂא Vah - Tee Shaw is נָשָׂא Naw Saw, meaning 'to Lift up', Notice that נָשָׂא Nee Saw which is spelled exactly the same means 'to be misled or to be deceived'. We realize that the Judges of The High Court felt like Moses and Aaron had deceived them. How did they come to this opinion? The Ten Spies spread malicious gossip about The Land and it's inhabitants. Bamidbar Rabah 9.18 - Was this what Moses spoke of when he said *'At That Time'*?

Now The Lord Appears to set the record straight. Moses and Aaron fell to the ground and began interceding for The People of Israel. Think about what is happening 'At That Time! All The People of Israel are angry with Moses and Aharon. They are making plans to return to Egypt, appoint a new Chief over them and to stone Joshua and Caleb. So where is Moses? He is bowed to the earth praying that The Lord would Forgive all B'nai Yisroel. See Numbers 14.11 -19. What a leader! The Lord did Forgive B'nei Yisroel but Prohibited those who sinned from entering The Land of Canaan.

Numbers 14.20 - 24
And the Lord Said, 'I Have Pardoned according to your word; However, as truly as I live, all the earth shall be filled with The Glory of The Lord. All those men which have seen everything from Aleph to Tav of My Glory, and My Miracles, which I Did in Egypt and in the

desert, and still have tested Me these ten times, and they have not listened to My voice; Surely they shall not see The Land which I Swore to their fathers, nor shall any of them who provoked Me see it; except for My servant Caleb, because he possessed a different spirit with him, and has followed Me fully. I shall bring him into The Land to which he came, and his seed shall possess it.'

B'nei Yisroel's rebellion resulted in the establishment of a Time / a Season for mourning. The High Court Ruled against Moses and Aharon. Their actions had repercussions!! The actions of The Sanhedrin misled The People of Israel. Their authority set in motion a day of great sadness and mourning that is incumbent upon each of us. Who wants to fast for Twenty-Six hours? Who wants to fast from sundown to sundown? Who wants to mourn? Yet, fasting and mourning are absolutely necessary to remind us to be very careful with those who lead us and for us who follow them. It is incumbent upon each of us to learn, and to know, each of the 613 Mitzvot of The Torah so that we can judge for ourselves what is the proper path to take. We must determine what is the correct course of action!

Numbers 14.22 - 23 makes it very clear that the men of B'nei Yisroel tested The Lord Ten times. They were Judged for repeated offenses. The Lord was Gracious and Merciful and Forgiving time and again as the offenses piled one upon the other. A picture should be beginning to emerge with regards to the Words *'At That Time'*.

Dear Ones, just Forty Days earlier Miriam was permitted to rejoin the camp of Israel after being separated for Seven Days. Remember, The Lord Descended in a pillar of cloud and stood at the entrance to The Tent of Meetings. The Lord Called to Aharon and Miriam. They appeared before The Lord. The Lord Spoke to them in the presence of all Israel. What did The Lord Say? This Teaching is important.

Numbers 13.6 - 10
And He Said, 'Listen to My Words; If there is a

Prophet among you, I, The Lord Will Make Myself known to him in a vision, and will speak to him in a dream. That is not the case with My servant Moses. He is the most trusted in all My House. I Speak mouth to mouth with him, in a vision, and not in riddles; and he gazes at the Likeness of The Lord, so why were you not afraid to speak against my servant Moses? And The Lord's Anger was kindled against them; and He Departed. And The Cloud Departed from atop The Tent; and, behold! Miriam had become leprous, white as snow; and Aharon looked towards Miriam, and, behold, she was leprous.'

The incident with The Prophetess Miriam was meant to be a lesson for each of us. Miriam was set outside of the encampment for Seven Days. All The People of Israel knew. The Sanhedrin knew. The Seventy Elders knew. All The People of Israel knew. The punishment of Miriam should have been fresh in their minds. Everyone should have remembered how The Lord Appeared in The Cloud and why The Prophetess Miriam became leprous and was separated from the encampment. How quickly we forget!

The actions of The Sanhedrin and The Seventy Elders were much more grievous than Miriam's in leading B'nei Yisroel to sin. We remember our failings and the failings of those who sinned on the 9th of Av. The failings of The Sanhedrin and B'nei Yisroel were not just for One Day. They are for The same Day each Year, Year after Year. Is this what Moses spoke of when he said 'At That Time'? Rabbi Nosson Scherman, The Stone Edition The Chumash (Mesorah Publications, Ltd., Brooklyn, N.Y. 1993), p. 803 - Rabbi Menachem M. Scheerson, Torah Chumash Shemot Kehot Publication Socierty (Brooklyn, NY 2006) p 86 - Avrohom Davis, Metsudah Midrash Tanchuma Bereishis 1 (Monsey, NY Eastern Book Press Inc. 2006) pp 296 - 297 - Rabbi Avrohom Davis, The Mesudah Chumash A New Linear Translation Bereishis (Hoboken New Jersey, KTVA Publishing House, Inc., 1991) p 178

Numbers 14.29 - 32

'Your carcasses shall fall in this wilderness; and all who were counted of you, according to your whole number, from twenty years old and upward, who have murmured against me, Shall by no means come into the land, concerning which I swore to make you live in it, save Caleb the son of Jephunneh, and Joshua the son of Nun. But your little ones, which you said should be a prey, them will I bring in, and they shall know the land which you have despised. But as for you, your carcasses, they shall fall in this wilderness.'

Some Teach that The Lord Instructed Moses to have The People of Israel travel to the Sea of Reeds. They base this on Numbers 14.25. I reviewed the original Language of Numbers 14.25 and do not see anything that Instructs B'nei Yisroel to travel to the Sea of Reeds. Numbers 14.25 ONLY instructs B'nei Yisroel to change the direction of the encampment from facing The Land of Israel to facing the wilderness and the path leading to the Sea of Reeds.

Numbers 14.25.

The Amalekites and the Canaanites live in the valley. Tomorrow you are to move and face the wilderness path towards the Sea of Reeds.

10 Av 2449

This is very significant because B'nei Yisroel did not travel anywhere. They remained in this location for 19 years. Rabbi Menachem M. Scheerson, Torah Chumash Shemot Kehot Publication Society (Brooklyn, NY 2006) p 89 Yet, The Holy Scripture notes them turning the direction of the camp without traveling. Why? This is an exact point of measurement in time. The 38 years of Deuteronomy 2.14 begins on the Day The Camp turned towards the wilderness facing the Sea of Reeds. The intent of The Words *'At That Time'* are based upon what happened then and each year on the same Day since.

This Day was the Day following the rebellion. This is The Day they went up the mountain to fight the Amalekites and Canaanites. They were crushed! See Deuteronomy Chapter One.

The last Verse in Deuteronomy Chapter One shares a very important nugget of Time with us.

Devarim 1.46
וַתֵּשְׁבוּ בְקָדֵשׁ יָמִים רַבִּים כַּיָּמִים אֲשֶׁר יְשַׁבְתֶּם׃

Deuteronomy 1.46
[ת - SIGN] *So you dwelled in Kadesh many Days,* [Years] *like the days* [Years] *you lived there* [elsewhere].

Again The Letter ת Tav appears in the Word וַתֵּשְׁבוּ to inform us to give a diligent search for in depth meaning. The intent is for us to discover that B'nei Yisroel dwelt in Kadesh for 19 years and wandered for 19 years. The Torah Informs us that the Time they dwelt was like the number of years when they wandered.

10 Av 2487 FC
Deuteronomy 2.14
And the Days from our leaving Kadesh-Barnea, until we came over the brook Zered, was thirty-eight years; until all the generation

of the men of war had perished from the camp, as the Lord swore to them.

The Thirty-Eight Years were measured to the exact Day, which was The Day after the 9th of Av. Remember that it was on the 9th of Av that the spies returned. Ten spies shared an evil report. B'nei Yisroel rebelled. This was Thirty-Eight Years from the next day. In addition to the text presented thus far, Holy Scripture Informs us 'all the generation of the men of war had perished from the camp'. On The 8th of Av the remaining men of war, about 15,000 dug their graves for the final time knowing they were the only ones left from the original 600,000 men of that generation. That night each of the remaining men of war perished from the Camp of B'nei Yisroel. The following morning was the 10th of Av 2487 FC.

After the last man of war had died It was 'At That Time' The Word of The Lord was fulfilled. 'all the generation of the men of war had perished from the camp, as the Lord swore to them.'

After the last man of war had died, Yisroel was divested of them. Their children were trained for war. They were ready to defeat Sicon and Og. '*At That Time*' is in reference to the final Day of the completion of the Thirty-Eight Years in which The people who rebelled died. There are Two Gematrias relating to The Number Thirty-Eight.

הָאֵבֶל
Haw Ay Vehl
The Mourning The Lamenting
38 = 30 ל   2 ב   1 א   5 ה

Each Year on the 9th of Av during the Thirty-Eight Year span of Judgment on those men who rebelled there was a great deal of mourning and lamenting as thousands died year after year. There was great bemoaning, bewailing, weeping and sadness as B'nei Yisroel revisited the 9th of Av each year.

יִבְכּוּ
Yee Vih Coo
To Mourn To Weep To Bewail
38 = 6 ו   20 כ   2 ב   10 י

1 Nissan 2487 FC
B'nei Yisroel arrives at Kodesh at the border to Edom.

10 Nissan 2487 FC
Miriam, the sister of Moses and Aharon, dies in a gentle, tranquil manner. It was like a kiss from The Creator. Miriam was buried there.

1 Av 2487 FC - Aharon Dies on Mt Hor - Numbers 33.38 - 39

7 Adar 2448 FC Moses our Teacher dies.

30 Av 2487 FC - B'nei Yisroel 30 Days of Mourning for Aharon ends. - Numbers 20.29 B'nei Yisroel defeated Sicon and Og.

Parshat Devarim Eikve
Deuteronomy 7.12 - 11.25

Chapter Three

Time Awareness

Dear Reader, the purpose of the discussion in Chapter Three is to draw our attention to Verses where Time is mentioned in The Weekly Parshat. It is so easy to pass through The Parshat time after time without giving much thought to Time. There are 111 Verses in Parshat Eikev. The Gematria of אֶלֶף Aleph is 111.

אֶלֶף
Aleph / One Thousand
111 = 80 ף 30 ל 1 א

סְאִים
Sih Eem / To Measure
111 = 40 ם 10 י 1 א 60 ס

The Letter א Aleph represents God. An Aleph

is One-Thousand. The Word סָאִים Sih Eem means to measure, The Gematria of Sih Eem is 111. It is like we are Mystically Instructed to measure The Verses of Eikev.

Our goal is to become more time conscience because Time is important in the Holy Scriptures. Time is a point of measurement. An Hour, a Day, a Week, a Month, and a Year are Measurements. Holy Days are measurements of Time. Time impacts Bible interpretation. It is easy to pass by measurements of Time without much thought.

On average, about every third Verse in Parshat Eikev mentions a form of Time. Some Verses, mention measurements of Time up to five times.

Let's begin by considering variations of the Word יוֹם Yohm, meaning Day in The Holy Scriptures.

יוֹם - Day

אַרְבָּעִים	יוֹם	וְאַרְבָּעִים	לַיְלָה
Ah Rih Baw Yeem	Yohn	Ah Rih Baw Yeem	Lah Yih Lawh
Forty	Day	And Forty	Night
323	56	329	75
883	616	889	

Deuteronomy 9.9
'When I went up to The Mount to receive The Tablets of Stone, The Tablets of The Covenant, which The Lord Made with you, then I stayed on The Mount Forty Days and Forty Nights. I did not eat bread nor drink water.'

Deuteronomy 9.11
'And it came to pass at the end of Forty Days and Forty Nights, that The Lord Gave me The Two Tablets of Stone, The Tablets of The Covenant.'

Deuteronomy 9.18
'And I fell down before The Lord, like the first, Forty Days and Forty Nights; I did not eat

bread, nor drink water, because of all your sins which you sinned, in doing wickedly in the sight of The Lord, to provoke Him to anger.'

Day and Night are singular in each of the above Verses. Translators translate Day as Days and Night as Nights. When translators do this, the reader is unaware. Moses was an educated man. There is a purpose for writing Forty Day and Forty Night. What is Moses sharing? Is Moses saying Forty Days was like a Day and Forty Nights was like A Night? What was it like for Moses when He was near The Lord God on Mount Sinai? We know that a Day with The Lord God is like a thousand Years to us. *'For a thousand years in Your sight is as yesterday,'* Psalm 90.4. Perhaps Moses is relating to us that Forty Days and Forty Nights was like a single Day and Night when in The Presence of The Lord God. Is Moses saying that One loses track of Time when in The Presence of The Lord God? Was Moses saying the Day and the Night blend into One? We know that with The Lord *'darkness is as light,'* Psalms 139.12.

Notice that Three of the Four Words we are discussing end with The Final Letter Mem. The Gematria of Mem is Forty. Two of The Words we are considering are Forty. Do we see anything unique with these Four Words?

What did Moses do when he was with The Lord God? The Lord God did not need Forty Days and Nights to write The Ten Commandments on Tablets of Stone. In Verse Eighteen Moses says he was *'fallen down before The Lord'*. Some translators say he was prostrated. However, וָאֶתְנַפַּל לִפְנֵי יְהֹוָה כָּרִאשֹׁנָה means Moses was *'fallen before The Lord like The First Time,'* Deuteronomy 9.18.

The Word אֶת Eht meaning 'Everything From Aleph to Tav' and נָפַל Nah Pahl meaning 'Fallen' are combined. Everything, i.e. Mind Body Soul were all fallen before The Lord. All of Moses faculties were fallen before The Lord. None of us understand what it is like to be fallen down before The Lord like Moses. Can we image lying face down on the ground with our hands and arms stretched out in front of our head for Forty Days and Nights like Moses? The Psalms helps us to understand what it was like for Moses.

Psalms 119.71
It is good for me that I have been afflicted; that I might learn your statutes.

Moses was afflicted. We associate affliction with fasting for twenty-six hours during Yom Kippur. Moses suffered to receive The Torah for us. Moses suffered to intercede for us. Moses was oppressed for us.

Psalm 6.9 - 10
Depart from me, all you evil doers; for The Lord Has heard the voice of my weeping. The Lord has heard my supplication; The Lord will receive my prayer.

Psalm 30.6 {KJV 5}
For His anger lasts but [1/16th of a second]; *in his favor is life; weeping may endure for an Evening / Night, but Joy Comes in the Morning / Day.*

First Moses Learned all The Words of The Torah. Second Moses interceeded. Third Moses again learned all The Words of The Torah. On Moses first and third ascent up Mount Sinai he received The Two Tablets of Stone inscribed by The Finger of The Lord and כְּכָל־הַדְּבָרִים אֲשֶׁר דִּבֶּר יְהוָה עִמָּכֶם 'all The Words that The Lord Spoke to You,' Deuteronomy 9.10. The Lord Taught Moses all 613 Observances of The Torah. In Chapter Two we learned that לְמַד Lee Mahd means to teach. We learned that the Gematria for לְמַד Lee Mahd was 74. In Psalms 119.71 The Word Lee Mahd, Learn, is spelled with an Aleph in front.

Our discussion began in this Chapter with the comment; The Letter א Aleph represents God. Mystically we Observe The Aleph in front of The Word לְמַד Lee Mahd. אֶלְמַד Eh Lih Mahd meaning, [The Lord] Teaches. The Gematria of אֶלְמַד Eh Lih Mahd and לַיְלָה Lah Yih Law meaning Night are 75.

לְמַד
Lee Mahd / To Teach
74 = 4 ד 40 מ 30 ל

לַיְלָה
Lah Yih Law
ל 30 י 10 נ 30 ה 5 = 75

אֱלְמַד
Eh Lih Mahd
א 1 ל 30 מ 40 ל 30 = 75

Mystically we Observe The Lord Taught Moses on Mount Sinai. Deuteronomy 10.10 has the same Four Words as the afore mentioned Verses plus Two additional Words.

יוֹם
Day

אַרְבָּעִים	יוֹם	וְאַרְבָּעִים	לַיְלָה
Ah Rih Baw Yeem	Yohn	Ah Rih Baw Yeem	Lah Yih Lawh
Forty	Day	And Forty	Night
323	56	329	75
883	616	889	

כַּיָּמִים
Like Days

	הָרִאשֹׁנִים	כַּיָּמִים
	Haw Ree Shoh Neem	Cah Yaw Meem
	The First	Like Days
	606	120
	1166	680

כַּיָּמִים הָרִאשֹׁנִים אַרְבָּעִים יוֹם וְאַרְבָּעִים לָיְלָה
'like the First Days, Forty Days and Forty Nights'

Deuteronomy 10.10
'And I stayed on the mount, like the First Days, Forty Days and Forty Nights; and The Lord Listened to me at that time also, and The Lord would not destroy you.'

In Deut 10.10 Moses adds the Words כַּיָּמִים הָרִאשֹׁנִים. Moses is comparing the Second Forty Day and Forty Night on Mount Sinai to the First Forty Day and Forty Night on Mount Sinai. He is saying the second is like the first. כַּיָּמִים Cah Yaw Meem means 'Like Days'.

Moses continues to use the singular Word for Day and Night even though in this Verse He identifies them as Days. This helps establish the point Moses is communicating a Mystical Message in Hebrew.

From this point on we are going to note some of the diverse references to Time. The reference to Time will first appear in Hebrew followed by the English translation followed by the Scriptures making this particular reference to Time. The screened Words in each Scripture are The Words associated with Time. We will go on for about Ten pages like this. The purpose is to show the many usages of Time in just One Parshat of Scripture.

בְּיוֹם

On The Day

Deuteronomy 9.10
'And The Lord Delivered to me Two Tablets of Stone written with The Finger of God; and on them was written according to all The Words, which The Lord Spoke with you in The Mount

out of the midst of The Fire on The Day of The Assembly.'

Deuteronomy 10.4
'And He Wrote on The Tablets, according to the First writing, The Ten Commandments, which The Lord Spoke to you on The Mount out of the midst of The Fire on The Day of the assembly; and The Lord Gave them to me.'

היום
The Day / This Day

Deuteronomy 8.1
'All The Commandments which I Command you This Day shall you take care to do, that you may live, and multiply, and go in and possess everything from Aleph to Tav of The Land which The Lord Swore to your fathers.'

Deuteronomy 8.11
'Beware that you forget not anything from Aleph to Tav of The Lord your God, in not Observing His Commandments, and His Judgments, and His Statutes, which I command

you This Day.'

Deuteronomy 8.19
'And it shall be, if you do forget The Lord your God, and walk after other gods, and serve them, and worship them, I warn you solemnly This Day that you shall surely perish.'

Deuteronomy 9.1
'Hear, O Israel; You are to pass over the Jordan This Day, to go in to possess nations greater and mightier than yourself, cities great and fortified up to heaven.'

Deuteronomy 9.3
'Understand therefore This Day, that The Lord your God is He who goes over before you; as a consuming fire He shall destroy them, and He shall bring them down before your face; so shall you drive them out, and destroy them quickly, as The Lord Has Said to you.'

Deuteronomy 9.7
'Remember, and forget not, how you provoked everything from Aleph to Tav of The Lord your

God to anger in the wilderness; from The Day when you departed out of The Land of Egypt, until you came to this place, you have been rebellious against The Lord.'

Deuteronomy 10.13
'To Observe The Commandments of The Lord, and His Statutes, which I Command you This Day for your good.'

Deuteronomy 11.2
'And know This Day; for I speak not with your children who have not known, and which have not seen the chastisement of The Lord your God, His Greatness, His Mighty Hand, and His Stretched out Arm.'

Deuteronomy 11.4
'And what He Did to the army of Egypt, to their horses, and to their chariots; how He Made the water of the Red Sea overflow them as they pursued after you, and how The Lord Has destroyed them until This Day.'

Deuteronomy 11.8
'Therefore shall you Observe everything from Aleph To Tav of all The Commandments which I Command you This Day, that you may be strong, and go in and possess The Land, which you are going over to possess.'

Deuteronomy 11.13
'And it shall come to pass, if you shall give heed diligently to My Commandments that I Command you This Day, to love The Lord your God and to serve Him with all your heart and with all your soul.'

Devarim 11.12
אֶרֶץ אֲשֶׁר־יְהֹוָה אֱלֹהֶיךָ דֹּרֵשׁ אֹתָהּ תָּמִיד עֵינֵי יְהֹוָה אֱלֹהֶיךָ בָּהּ מֵרֵשִׁית הַשָּׁנָה וְעַד אַחֲרִית שָׁנָה:

Deuteronomy 11.12
'A Land which The Lord your God Cares for; The Eyes of The Lord your God are always upon it, from the beginning of The Year to the end of The Year.'

כַּיּוֹם
Like The Day

Deuteronomy 8.18
'And you shall remember The Lord your God; for He is who gives you power to get wealth, that He may establish His Covenant that He Swore to your fathers, as it is This Day.'

Deuteronomy 10.15
'Only The Lord Took delight in your fathers to love them, and He Chose their seed after them, you above all people, as it is This Day.'

כָּל־הַיָּמִים
All The Days

Deuteronomy 11.1
'Therefore you shall love The Lord your God, and keep His Charge, and His Statutes, and His Judgments, and His Commandments, All The Days.'

מִיוֹם
From The Day

Deuteronomy 9.24
'You have been rebellious against the Lord from The Day that I knew you.'

מַהֵר
Quickly

Deuteronomy 7.22
'And The Lord your God will clear away those nations before you, little by little; you may not destroy them quickly, lest the beasts of the field grow numerous upon you.'

מָיִם
This Day

Deuteronomy 11.11
'Beware that you forget not the Lord your God, in not keeping His Commandments, and His Judgments, and His Statutes, which I command you This Day.'

אַרְבָּעִים שָׁנָה
Forty Years

Deuteronomy 8.2
'And you shall remember everything from Aleph to Tav of all the way which The Lord your God led you these Forty Years in the wilderness, to humble you, and to prove you, to know what was in your heart, whether you would Observe His Commandments, or not.'

Deuteronomy 8.4
'Your garment did not grow old upon you, nor did your foot swell, these Forty Years.'

בְּאַחֲרִיתֶךָ
In Your End

Deuteronomy 8.16
'Who fed you in the wilderness with manna, which your fathers knew not, that He might humble you, and that He might test you, to do you good in the end.'

בַּפַּעַם הַהִוא
At That Time

Deuteronomy 9.19
'For I was afraid of the anger and hot displeasure, with which The Lord was Angry with you to destroy you. But The Lord Listened to me at that time also.'

בָּעֵת
At That Time

Deuteronomy 9.20
'And The Lord was so very angry with Aaron that he was ready to destroy him, and I prayed for Aaron also at that time.'

Deuteronomy 10.8
'At that time The Lord Set apart The Tribe of Levi, to carry The Ark of The Covenant of The Lord, to stand before The Lord to minister to him, and to bless in His Name, to this day.'

יְמֵיכֶם וִימֵי
Your Days And the Days

Deuteronomy 11.21
'That your days may be multiplied, and the days of your children, in The Land, which The Lord swore to your fathers to give them, as The Days of heaven upon the earth'.

מַהֵר
Quickly

Deuteronomy 9.12
And The Lord Said to me, 'Arise, get down quickly from here; for your people, which you have brought out of Egypt, have corrupted themselves; they have quickly turned aside from the way which I Commanded them; they have made themselves a molten image.'

Deuteronomy 9.16
'And I looked, and, behold, you had sinned against The Lord your God, and had made yourselves a molten calf; you had turned aside quickly from the way which The Lord Had Commanded you.'

הָרִאשֹׁנִים
The First

Deuteronomy 10.2
'And I will write on The Tablets The Words that were in The First Tablets that you broke, and you shall put them in The Ark.'

אֶת־אַרְבָּעִים הַיּוֹם וְאֶת־אַרְבָּעִים הַלַּיְלָה
Everything from Aleph to Tav of Forty Days and everything from Aleph to Tav of Forty Nights,

Deuteronomy 9.25
'Thus, I fell down before The Lord everything from Aleph to Tav of Forty Days and everything from Aleph to Tav of Forty Nights, because the Lord had Said He would destroy you.'

The יוֹם Yohm Table

Below are Sixteen different ways to spell Day in Hebrew, This sounds confusing but it's easy once the reader memorizes how to spell Yohm.

Name	שֵׁם	ב	ה	ו	כ	ל	מ
	Name	In	The	And	Like	To	From
Day	יוֹם	בַּיוֹם	הַיוֹם	וְיוֹם	כַּיוֹם	לַיוֹם	מִיוֹם
	241	523	458	15	42	46	25

	שֵׁם	וב	וה		וכ	ול	ומ
	Name	And in	And the		And like	And to	And from
Day	יוֹם	וּבַיוֹם	וְהַיוֹם		וּכְיוֹם	וּלְיוֹם	וּמִיוֹם
	241	56	6		1	1	1

On The Day	From The Days	From The Day	And The Day
כִּימֵי	יְמֵיכֶם	מֵהַיוֹם	וִימֵי
4	1	3	3

Parshat Devarim Re'ey
Deuteronomy 11.26 - 16.17

Chapter Four
Specific Direction of Time And Gematria

Day 1 Month 11 Year 2488 FC

Dear Ones, I am deeply intrigued by the Seventy-Four usages of The Word הַיּוֹם Ha Yohm meaning 'This Day' or 'Today' in Deuteronomy. Each usage of Ha Yohm is a reference to a place and point in Time. Mystically, each of the Seventy-Four references to Time in Deuteronomy is a learning portal. The Word דַּע Daha means 'Know'. The common usage for דַּע is יְדַע. The Gematria for דַּע is Seventy-Four.

דַּע
Dah / Know
74 = 70 ע 4 ד

Here we mystically observe Time and Gematria. Each time הַיּוֹם Ha Yohm is written in Deuteronomy gold nuggets of knowledge are waiting to be discovered. This is the purpose for writing this book. Let's take this a step further. Each time הַיוֹם Ha Yohm is written in Ha Torah there are gold nuggets of knowledge to be understood. Each time הַיוֹם is written in Ha Torah we are to congregate around הַיוֹם to learn. We are to assemble around הַיוֹם. The Word הַיוֹם Ha Yohm is written 135 times in Ha Torah. The Gematria for קְהַל meaning 'Congregation or Assembly' is 135. Note Exodus 12.6 says, כֹּל קְהַל עֲדַת־יִשְׂרָאֵל - *'All The Assemble of Witnesses among Yisroel'*.

קְהַל
Kih Hahl Assembly
135 = 30 ל 5 ה 100 ק

Like The Word עֵת Ayt in Chapter One and יוֹם in Chapter Three, each usage can be representative of a gold nugget in Time. In Chapter Two we learned that The Word בָּעֵת Baw Ayt represented Thirty Eight Years. In Chapter Three we learned that יוֹם represented Forty Days and Forty Nights. Here in Chapter

Four we learn, God Willing, that every time הַיּוֹם is written in The Torah, we should stop, set up camp and learn for awhile.

Before we continue learning, I would like us to note the Five usages of הַיּוֹם in this Parshat.

Devarim 12.8

לֹא תַעֲשׂוּן כְּכֹל אֲשֶׁר אֲנַחְנוּ עֹשִׂים פֹּה הַיּוֹם אִישׁ כָּל־הַיָּשָׁר בְּעֵינָיו:

Deuteronomy 12.8
You shall not do after all the things that we do here this day, every man whatever is right in his own eyes.

Devarim 13.19

כִּי תִשְׁמַע בְּקוֹל יְהֹוָה אֱלֹהֶיךָ לִשְׁמֹר אֶת־כָּל־מִצְוֹתָיו אֲשֶׁר אָנֹכִי מְצַוְּךָ הַיּוֹם לַעֲשׂוֹת הַיָּשָׁר בְּעֵינֵי יְהֹוָה אֱלֹהֶיךָ:

Deuteronomy 13.19
When you give heed to The Voice of The Lord your God, to Observe all His Commandments that I Command you This Day and do that which is right in The Eyes of The Lord your God.

Devarim 15.5

רַק אִם־שָׁמוֹעַ תִּשְׁמַע בְּקוֹל יְהֹוָה אֱלֹהֶיךָ לִשְׁמֹר לַעֲשׂוֹת אֶת־כָּל־הַמִּצְוָה הַזֹּאת אֲשֶׁר אָנֹכִי מְצַוְּךָ הַיּוֹם:

Deuteronomy 15.5
Only if you carefully listen to The Voice of The Lord your God, to take care to do all these Commandments that I Command you This Day.

Devarim 15.15

וְזָכַרְתָּ כִּי עֶבֶד הָיִיתָ בְּאֶרֶץ מִצְרַיִם וַיִּפְדְּךָ יְהֹוָה אֱלֹהֶיךָ עַל־כֵּן אָנֹכִי מְצַוְּךָ אֶת־הַדָּבָר הַזֶּה הַיּוֹם: טז

Deuteronomy 15.15
And you shall remember that you were a slave in the land of Egypt, and The Lord your God Redeemed you; therefore I Command you This Today.

There are many uniquenesses throughout Deuteronomy. For example, The Words אָנֹכִי מְצַוְּךָ Aw Noh Cee - Mih Tzah Vih Kawh meaning 'I Command You' occur Twenty Six times in Deuteronomy. We know that The Holy Name for The Lord, which we do not say aloud, is the Gematria of Twenty Six.

י ה ו ה
The Lord
26 = 5 ה 6 ו 5 ה 10 י

We make an additional observation. Notice that The Word הַיּוֹם is added to the above Two Words. אָנֹכִי מְצַוְּךָ הַיּוֹם Aw Noh Cee - Mih Tzah Vih Kawh - Hah Yohm meaning 'I Command You Today' is written Eighteen times in Deuteronomy. These Three Hebrew Words put a definition to The Time and The Gematria. What are we to make of this? We will camp out around these Words for a little while.

We know that The Observances in The First Four Books Of Moses, i.e. Genesis, Exodus, Leviticus and Numbers were given by The Lord God on Mt Sinai. The Lord Instructed Moses to Teach The People of Israel the last 245 Observances in Deuteronomy during his last Thirty-Six Days as noted below.

Deuteronomy 1.3
And it happened in Year Forty in Month Eleven, in Day One to the Month that Moses

shared with The People of Israel, about every Command that The Lord Said to him with them.

Deuteronomy 4.40
Therefore, You shall keep His Statutes, and His Commandments, which I Command you Today, that it may go well with you, and with your children after you, and that you may prolong your days upon The Land, which The Lord your God Gives you, forever.

Deuteronomy 1.3 informs us that *'It was in Year Forty, Month Eleven and the first Day that Moses Spoke to The People of Israel'*. This was Thirty-Seven Days from The Day Moses died. Moses died on Day Seven of Month Twelve, i.e. the 7th of Adar. He did not Teach B'nei Yisroel on the day of his death. Moses taught us Thirty-Six Days from Deuteronomy 1.3 until 6 Adar. Rabbi Nosson Scherman, The Stone Edition The Chumash (Mesorah Publications, Ltd., Brooklyn, N.Y. 1993), p. 939; Heninrich W. Guggenheimer, Seder Olam {A Jason Aronson Book, Lanham,

Maryland, Rowman & Littlefield Publishers, Inc. 2005) p 100

In addition to knowing when Moses began these Instructions we notice there are break periods amidst The Instruction. Where are the break points? Each time Moses Said the Words אָנֹכִי מְצַוְּךָ הַיּוֹם Aw Noh Cee - Mih Tzah Vih Kawh - Hah Yohm meaning 'I Command You Today', there is a break. Please note the before mentioned Verses of Deuteronomy 13.19 and 15.5. There is no point for Moses to Say 'I command you 'This Day' more than once. Why repeat 'I Command you This Day if he has already said it? So when Moses Says, 'I Command You This Day' it concludes an instruction or begins an instruction. The periods of instruction average out to about Two Days each. 36 divided by 2 = 18. Again, The Words, 'I Command you This Day' are written Eighteen times in Deuteronomy. Eighteen represents 'Life' The Observances of Ha Torah are to bring us life! When we follow the Instructions of The Torah they, prolong our life.

חַי
Chai Live / Life
18 = 10 , 8 ח

When we examine the entire Book of Deuteronomy, we will discover these periods of learning. In Parshat Re'ey, There are 54 Observances. Seventeen are Performative and thirty-seven are prohibitive.　Rabbi A. Y. Kahan The Taryag Mitzvot (Brooklyn, N.Y. Keser Torah Publications　1987, 1988) p 266

Devarim 15.7

כִּי־יִהְיֶה בְךָ אֶבְיוֹן מֵאַחַד אַחֶיךָ בְּאַחַד שְׁעָרֶיךָ בְּאַרְצְךָ אֲשֶׁר־יְהֹוָה אֱלֹהֶיךָ נֹתֵן לָךְ לֹא תְאַמֵּץ אֶת־לְבָבְךָ וְלֹא תִקְפֹּץ אֶת־יָדְךָ מֵאָחִיךָ הָאֶבְיוֹן:

Deuteronomy 15.7
If there is among you a poor man of one of your brothers, inside any of your gates, in your land, which the Lord your God gives you, you shall not harden your heart, nor shut your hand from your poor brother.

לְבָבְךָ
Lih Vaw Veh Kah
Your Heart
54 = 20 ךְ 2 בָ 2 בְ 30 לְ

What are we to take away from our discussion? All the Mitzvot are to assist us in how we behave. What do we pray everyday?

Deuteronomy 6.5 - 6
And you shall love the Lord your God with all your heart, and with all your soul, and with all your might. And these words, which I command you this day, shall be in your heart.

Parshat Devarim Shoftim
Deuteronomy 16.18 - 21.9

Chapter Five
The Time of First Fruits

Dear Ones, We are going to discuss several Observances specific to The Land of Israel and their relationship to The End of Days in this Chapter. These Observances are linked ONLY to the Land of Israel. ONLY those Jews living in The Land Of Israel can perform these Observances. Those of us outside the Land of Israel should not ignore these Mitzvot. We should be aware of them. We should be supportive of them even though we who are outside The Land of Israel cannot perform them.

Has anyone stopped to consider why The Land of Israel is called 'The Holy Land?' There are a number of possible answers to the question.

From all within creation, The Lord God Took this universe, this world and especially The

Land of Israel as The Place to put His Name. Then The Lord God Separated The Land of Israel from all other lands, worlds, and universes through Mitzvot, i.e. Observances. When The Lord God Separated The Seventh Day from the other Six Days The Seventh Day became Holy. The Seventh Day is unlike the other Six Days.

Exodus 20.8
Remember The Sabbath Day, to keep it Holy.

Why?

Exodus 20.9 -
Six Days shall you labor, and do all your work! But. The Seventh Day is The Sabbath of The Lord your God. In it you shall not do any work, neither you, nor your son, nor your daughter, your manservant, nor your maidservant, nor your cattle, nor your stranger that is within your gates. For in Six Days The Lord Made The Heaven and earth, the sea, and all that is in them, and Rested on The Seventh Day. Therefore The Lord Blessed The Sabbath Day and Made it Holy.

We see how The Lord God Made The Seventh Day Holy. He Separated The Seventh Day from the other Six Days.

The People of Israel are Holy.

Why?

Exodus 19.6
You have seen what I did to the Egyptians, and how I Carried you on eagles' wings and Brought you to Myself. Now therefore, if you will obey My Voice indeed, and keep My Covenant, then you shall be My own treasure among all peoples; for all the earth is mine. And you shall be to Me a kingdom of Priests, and a Holy Nation.

The Lord God Separated The People of Israel from all the other nations by Giving them Mitzvot / Observances to follow.

Deuteronomy 7.6

For you are a holy people to the Lord your God; the Lord your God has chosen you to be a special people to himself, above all peoples that are upon the face of the earth.

The Priests are Holy, The garments of the Priests are Holy. The Mishkan / Tabernacle is Holy. The items in the Tabernacle / Temple are Holy. The Altar is Holy. The Utensils are Holy. The Offerings are Holy. The Menorah is Holy. The Ark is Holy. The Holy Place is Holy. The city of Jerusalem is Holy.

The Land of Israel is Holy.

How do we know this?

Deuteronomy 23.16
For The Lord your God Walks in the midst of your camp, to save you, and to give your enemies to you. Therefore, your camp, i.e. dwelling place / Land shall be Holy; that he should see no unclean thing in you, and turn away from you.
We also know The Land of Israel is Holy

because many Mitzvot, i.e. Commands in The Torah are regarding The Land. We will consider a few of the Observances that separate The Land of Israel from all other Lands.

Dear Ones, our discussion in this chapter will be a little like a hexagon. The heart of our discussion is Deuteronomy 18.3 - 5. We will branch off from our discussion several times then return.

On the Day, Moses taught the Observance known as 'The Great Triumph' The People of Israel were living outside of The Land of Israel. Before anyone could perform this Observance The Land of Israel had to be conquered and divided. Then Jewish farmers would need to settle in The Land and plant grain, grape vineyards and olive trees. Vineyards and olive trees remained because The Army of Israel was prohibited from cutting down fruit trees in Deuteronomy 20.19.

Deuteronomy 18.1 - 5

The Priests the Levites, and all The Tribe of Levi shall have no part nor inheritance with Israel; they shall eat The Offerings of The Lord made by fire, and His inheritance. Therefore shall they have no inheritance among their brothers; The Lord is their inheritance, as He Has Said to them. 'And this shall be The Priest's due from The People, from those who offer a sacrifice, whether it is ox or sheep; and they shall give to The priest the shoulder, and the two cheeks, and the stomach. Also The firstfruit of your grain, of your wine, and of your oil, and the first of the fleece of your sheep, shall you give to him.' For The Lord your God has chosen him out of all your tribes, to stand to minister in The Name of The Lord, him and his sons FOREVER.

Two Mitzvot
There are two Mitzvot in Deuteronomy 18.1 - 2. Both are Prohibitive Observances. The First Observance is in regards to the Kohanim / Priests. *'The Priests the Levites, and all The Tribe of Levi shall have no part nor inheritance with Israel'*. This means The Tribe

of Levi will not inherit a section of The Land of Eretz Yisroel except for the Forty-Eight Cities. [Leviticus 25.34 and Numbers 35.27]. The second Observance is The Tribe of Levi could not share in the booty the armies of Israel captured during their conquest.

We are going to branch off for several pages to discuss Three Mitzvot associated with The Cities and The Land given to The Levites as an inheritance.

Numbers 35.1 - 7
And The Lord Spoke to Moses in the plains of Moab by the Jordan at Jericho, Saying; 'Command The People of Israel, that they give to The Levites of the inheritance of their possession cities to live in. And you shall also give to The Levites an open ground around the cities. And they shall have the cities to live in, and their open ground shall be for their cattle, and for their goods, and for all their beasts. And the open ground around the cities, that you shall give to The Levites, shall reach from the wall of the city outward a thousand cubits

around. And you shall measure from outside the city on the east side Two Thousand cubits, and on the south side Two Thousand cubits, and on the west side Two Thousand cubits, and on the north side Two thousand cubits and the city shall be in the midst. This shall be to them the open ground of the cities. And the cities that you shall give to the Levites shall be six cities of refuge, which you shall appoint for the man slayer that he may flee there; and to them you shall add Forty Two cities. So all the cities that you shall give to The Levites shall be Forty Eight cities; both them and their open grounds.'

The Levites and the Priests are separated unto The Lord. The Tribe of Levi is a chosen Tribe from among the other Tribes of Israel. They are separated for and dedicated to service in and around the Holy Temple. They are to spend their time studying and Teaching Ha Torah. They are also The Learning Centers distributed throughout The Land of Israel where by their brethren may come to study. Six of the cites are cites of refuge for one who has accidentally murdered to flee to for protection. This is a Pro-formative Mitzvah.

Leviticus 25.34
But the field of the pasture lands of their cities may not be sold; for it is their everlasting possession.

Mitzvah
There is a great deal more to this Mitzvah than what we will discuss. I am sharing Two Mitzvot to help us better realize the permanency of The last Word in Deuteronomy 18.5, *'FOREVER.'* The FOREVER is complicated in this sense. Deuteronomy 18.1-5 Informs us that The People of Israel are to give to The Levites 'A due' forever. How can we Observe this Command today? It is challenging!

Mitzvah
We are also informed in Numbers 35.2 - 7 that The People of Israel are to give Forty-Eight Cities to The Levites along with The Land surrounding each city going out Two-Thousand

Cubits. A cubit is between eighteen to Twenty-One inches in length. This means between 3,000 to 3,500 feet. Now we must inquire which are the Forty-Eight cities? Are the Forty-Eight cities still in existence today? I don't know.

Mitzvah
In Leviticus 25.34 The Torah Informs us of another Mitzvah. The Land surrounding the Forty-Eight Cities cannot be altered or sold. In this age, it is likely that some of the land surrounding the Forty-Eight cities has been sold.

Here is where it becomes complicated! The Forty-Eight cities must be returned to The Levites. The land around these cities must be returned to The Levities. Who owns the homes in theses cities? How expensive are these homes? What has happened to The Land around these cities? Has The Land been sold? Has The Land been altered? For us, this is a big mess. Yet, these are Three Mitzvot of Ha Torah with 'FOREVER' stamped on them By

The Lord God! How are these Three Observances related to our discussion?

We now return to where we began our discussion. Moses was Teaching The People of Israel in The Year 2488 FC. The People of Israel were just a short time from beginning the conquest of Eretz Yisroel. Moses was explaining these Mitzvot with an eye on when they would be fulfilled years down the road.

Dear Ones, this is where we are at today. We are 3,287 years from when Moses spoke these Words. The Jewish people do not occupy all of The Land Promised to them by The Lord God. Millions of Jews live outside of Eretz Yisroel. The Levites do not occupy the Forty-Eight Cities as intended in Scripture. The Land outside the Forty-Eight cities has been altered. I am saying the Mitzvot spoken of in the above Scriptures will need to be reestablished again as it was in the Days of Joshua!

Prophecy

There will be a serious war to reclaim our land. Jews from every corner of the world will come to help liberate The Land of Israel Again. Perhaps, Some countries will be wiped off the face of the earth. Moshiach / Messiah will lead forces to defeat all our enemies. This time, they will be defeated once and for all! I am saying The People of Israel will fight these wars at The End of Days as they fought these wars again in the days of Joshua. So it is like each of us is standing before the great Prophet Moses hearing His Words again 3,287 Years later.

We return to the subject at hand.

2488 FC
Once the Land of Israel was conquered, Jewish farmers settled the land and planted crops of grain, i.e. wheat, oats, rye, barley, and spelt. Then they could harvest their First Fruits. When a Jewish farmer owned land with grape vines or olive trees they could observe the Mitzvah of offering First Fruits without planting them first..

Mitzvah

Another Observance for The Land of Israel is The Shmittah Year. Every Seventh Year The Land of Israel is to be given a Time of rest. This Year, 5775 FC From Creation is a Shmittah Year. The Shmittah Year began on Rosh HaShanah, Sept 25, 2014, and continued until September 13, 2015. In conjunction with the Shmittah Year is The Release of debt between The People of Israel. Deuteronomy 15.1 - 3.

The forgiveness of debt is measured according to The Shmittah Year.

Deuteronomy 15.1 - 3
At the end of every Seven Years, you shall grant a release. And, this is the manner of the release. Every creditor who lends anything to his neighbor shall release it. He shall not exact it of his neighbor, or of his brother; because it is called The Lord's Release. Of a foreigner, you may exact it again, but that which is yours with your brother your hand shall release.

The above Scriptures contain Three Mitzvot.

They are:

Mitzvah
An Individual of B'nei Yisroel that is owed money from another individual of B'nei Yisroel may not demand payment of money owed once the Shmittah has passed. This Mitzvah is Observed in The Land of Israel.

Mitzvah
The Lord God Commands that the debt be 100% forgiven. Those of B'nei Yisroel who are owed money from B'nai Yisroel must write a waiver saying I waive all claims to debts owed me from among The People of Israel.

Mitzvah
There is a separation between the People of Israel and The People of Noach. Debts owed to anyone among B'nei Yisroel may demand payment from among The People of B'nai Noach when the debts are due regardless of The Shmittah year.

The Mitzvah is ONLY for The People of Israel.

Why mention The Release? The Release happens in conjunction with the Seventh Year. At nightfall on September 13, 2015, all debt among The People of Israel living in Israel was canceled.

When the last day of Elul 5775 FC From Creation concludes The Shmittah Year ends. . This is also the last Day of the Seventh Year. All debt between B'nei Yisroel is canceled with the exception of the debt assigned to the Bet Din, i.e. Jewish Court.

During The Shmittah Year The Land of Israel sits. There is no plowing. There is no sowing of seed. There is no harvesting for profit.

Leviticus 25.20 - 22
And if you shall say, What shall we eat the seventh year? Behold, we shall not sow, nor gather in our produce; Then I Will Command My Blessing upon you in the sixth year, and it shall bring forth fruit for three years. And you shall sow the eighth year, and eat still of old fruit until the ninth year; until its fruits come in

you shall eat of the old store.

The Torah is not saying that The People Living on The Land in Israel must go three years complete years without sowing or harvesting. Here is what The Torah is Saying. Our present Shmittah year began 01 Tishrei 5775 F.C. However in reality it began much earlier. Farmers would only plant crops that they could harvest before The Shmittah began.

5774 FC
We count this year Farmers could only harvest crops up to when The Shmittah year begins. Farmers could not plant fall crops because The Shmittah Year began. All work on The Land stopped when The Shmittah year began.

5775 FC
No planting sowing, fertilizing or harvesting was done during The Shmittah Year. The Land rested.

5776 FC
The Last Day of Elul 5775 FC concludes The Shmittah Year. However with all The Holy

Observances that begin with The new Year planting among The People of Israel would not begin until the spring. Why?

2 Mitzvot
Deuteronomy 16.16
Three times in a year all your males shall appear before The Lord your God in The Place, which he shall choose [Jerusalem. You shall appear] at The Feast of Unleavened Bread, and at The Feast of Weeks, and at The Feast of Booths. And [The Men among The People of Israel] shall not appear before The Lord empty. Every man shall give as he is able, according to the blessing of The Lord your God which He Has Given you.

Mitzvah
The Second Mitzvot is appearing with an offering. We are to give as The Lord as He Has Blessed us. If the blessing is tiny, then a small gift is appropriate. If the blessing is great, then a large gift is appropriate.

3,287 years ago this meant traveling by foot,

donkey or camel to Jerusalem. In some instances, several weeks of traveling was necessary to arrive in time to build a booth to celebrate the Festival of Booths.

As a way of example, The journey to Jerusalem by a descendant from The Tribe of Simeon living is southern Israel would be about 140 miles {225 KM} as the eagle flies. Traveling by foot may have required a journey through dessert or up over mountains etc. which were the common method of travel.

The length of a days journey was about 15 miles. Merrill C. Tenney, General Editor, The Zondervan Pictorial Encyclopedia of the Bible Volume Five (Grand Rapids MI Zondervan Publishing House 3rd printing 1978) p 799. The average traveler would take about nine days each way. However, when one includes the Observance of not traveling on Shabbat, it is likely that the Nine Days journey becomes a Twelve Day journey depending on Shabbat and other High Holy Days.

As a way of example, if a descendant of Dan living in northern Israel were to travel to Jerusalem the journey would be about 100 miles {150 KM}. This would require about Six Days each way. When one includes the Observance of not traveling on Shabbat or High Holy Days the Six Day journey becomes perhaps a Nine Day journey.

Remember, we are discussing why the Jewish farmer may not sow his fields immediately after the Shmittah Year. All the men of age are in Jerusalem for the Observances of Rosh Hashanah, The Ten Days of Repentance and Yom Kippur followed by the Festival of Booths. There is not enough time to travel home and to then return for The Festival of Booths. If the men were to travel when they arrived home, there would be little time available for preparing the fields for planting and sowing the fields.

We learn from these examples that Time plays a crucial part in why farmers do not plant their fields immediately after Rosh Ha Shanah ends.

Even though The Torah Does not discuss the Time factor, the reader can see why time is a big factor.

When we read רֵאשִׁית דְּגָנְךָ in Deuteronomy 18.1 - 5, meaning,'Your First Grain' we should realize this is about the First Day of The Festival of Weeks, Shavuot. We connect the Time, with the Festival of Shavuot.

Numbers 28.26
Also on the Day of The Firstfruits when you bring a new Grain Tribute to The Lord on your Festival of Weeks it shall be a Holy Gathering to you. Cease all labors / work.

What we just discussed about traveling also applies here. It would be difficult to travel home after the conclusion of the Festival of Matzah and to return a few weeks later. Most men stayed the from Passover until the conclusion of Shavuot. Including the traveling Time, this could be as long as eighty days. Understanding the Time and travel issues helps us also to understand why parts of Three Years are required when Observing the Shmittah Year.

Another point is that after all battles were fought, and the wars won, and The People of Israel were entirely in possession of The Land of Israel, and then The Land was divided. After The Land had been divided, The Jewish farmers planted wheat in the spring. Some of the new Wheat [Grains] were first brought to The Lord on Shavuot / The Festival of Weeks / Pentecost.

Dear Reader, Moses died on the 7th of Adar 2488 FC. The People of Israel mourned for Moses for Thirty Days until the 7th of Nissan 2488. Joshua Instructed the People they would be crossing the Jordan in three Days on the 10th of Nissan. The People of Israel crossed the Jordan River, then journeyed to the eastern edge of Jericho and camped at Gilgal.

10 Nissan 2488 FC
Joshua 4.19
And the people came up out of the Jordan on

the Tenth Day of the First Month, and encamped in Gilgal, in the east border of Jericho.

Joshua performs Brit Milah / Circumcision on all the males. On the 14th of Nissan at eve the People of Israel celebrate their first Passover in The Holy Land.

14 Nissan 2488 FC
Joshua 5.9 - 11
And the Lord Said to Joshua, 'This day have I rolled away the reproach of Egypt from off you.' Therefore, the name of the place is called Gilgal to this day. And The people of Israel encamped in Gilgal and kept the Passover on the fourteenth day of the month in the evening in the plains of Jericho. And they ate of the old grain of the land on the next day after the Passover, unleavened cakes, and parched grain in the same day.

Joshua 14.6-10
Then the sons of Judah came to Joshua in Gilgal; and Caleb the son of Jephunneh the

Kenazite said to him, 'You know the thing that The Lord Said to Moses the man of God concerning me and you in Kadesh-Barnea. I was Forty years old when Moses the servant of The Lord sent me from Kadesh-Barnea to spy out The land; [29 Sivan 2449 FC] and I brought him back word as it was in my heart. And my brothers who went up with me made the heart of the people melt; but I wholly followed the Lord my God. And Moses swore on that day, [9 Av 2449 FC] saying, Surely the land on which your feet have trodden shall be your inheritance, and your children's forever, because you have wholly followed the Lord my God. And now, behold, the Lord Has Kept me alive, as He Said, these forty-five years, since The Lord spoke this word to Moses, while the people of Israel wandered in the wilderness; and now, behold, I am this day eighty-five years old [29 Sivan 2495 FC].

Our Sages Teach that The Conquest for The Land of Israel took Seven Years. It is based on this text. Caleb was Forty Years of age when the spies were sent. This was the second year in the Wilderness. Add Thirty-Eight Years to Forty Years. When B'nei Yisroel began the conquest for The Land of Israel Caleb was 78 Years old. Now we move ahead to Joshua 14.6 - 10. Caleb says he is 85 Years old. This informs us that the conquest took Seven Years. 78 from 85 = 7.

The Seventh Year was the Shmittah Year [2495 FC]. This was The First Seven Years in the Jubilee count of Forty-Nine Years. Ninety Days later The Shmittah Year would end with the beginning of the New Year 01 Tishri 2496 FC.

Farmers were not plowing their fields yet. The task of dividing the Land among The Twelve Tribes begins. This is why Caleb came to Joshua. He wanted to insure that The Tribe of Judah received the city of Hebron. How long did the division of The Land of Israel take? Our Sages teach Seven years? How do we know this? Remember back to Chapter Two where we discussed the meaning of 'Many Days' regarding the Nineteen Years the People of Israel lived in Kadesh. In Joshua 22.23 we have another use of many Days.

Joshua 22.1 - 4
Then Joshua called the Reubenites, and the Gadites, and half the tribe of Manasseh, And said to them, You have kept all that Moses the servant of The Lord commanded you and have obeyed my voice in all that I commanded you; You have not left your brothers these many days to this day, [01 Nissan 2502 FC] but have kept the charge of the commandment of the Lord your God. And now the Lord your God Has Given rest to your brothers, as he promised them. Therefore, now return, and go to your tents, and to The Land of your possession, which Moses, the servant of The Lord, gave you on the other side of the Jordan.

These Many Days means the division of the land required Seven Years. So the first Seven Years the army of Israel conquered The Holy Land. Then the second Seven Years The Holy Land was divided. The division of the Holy Land concluded about ninety days from the completion of the second Shmittah year. The second Seven Year period ended with the Shmittah Year [2502 FC]. This was the second Seven Years in the Jubilee count of Forty-Nine Years. 01 Tishri 2503 FC began which is September in the Gregorian Calendar. Now farmers were free to prepare their land for sowing wheat and other produce. After The Festival of Booths, the wheat crop was sown in the spring of 2503 FC. The first festival which new grain was offered by farmers from all twelve Tribes was Shavuot 2503 FC. This was a little over fourteen years from when Moses spoke the Words רֵאשִׁית דְּגָנְךָ 'Your First Grain'.

דְּגָנְךָ
Dih Gaw Nih Kah / Your Grain
77 = 20 ךְ 50 נ 3 ג 4 ד

It is like the first Seven represents the Seven Years of conquest for the Holy Land of Israel and the second Seven is for the division of The Holy Land Of Israel. Seven plus Seven.

The Seventy-Seven is significant because it

points to the Altar The Tribes of Ruben and Gad along with half The Tribe of Manasseh constructed after returning to their tents in Joshua 22. The armies from The Ten Tribes of Israel gathered to war against them because of that altar. However, The Ten Tribes learned the altar was not intended for sacrifice. It was intended to be a testimony to their children of the Victories The Lord Brought. The Gematria for sacrifice and for 'your altar' are both 77.

מִזְבַּחֲךָ
Meez Bah Chah Kaw / Your Altar
77 = 20 ךָ 8 ח 2 ב 7 ז 40 מ

זִבְחֲכֶם
Zee Bih Chah Chawm / Sacrifice
77 = 40 ם 20 כ 8 ח 2 ב 7 ז

רֵאשִׁית
Rah Sheet / First
911 = 400 ת 10 י 300 שׁ 1 א 200 ר
Some have inquired about the significance of 911 occurring during a Shmittah year. 9-11-2001 was during the Shmittah Year in 5761

FC. From Creation. The Shmittah ended on September 18, 2001. The Shmittah is only in relation to The Land of Israel. 2008 was a Shmittah Year. 2015 is a Shmittah Year.

I cannot predict what enemies plan or do. All that I can say is that the Shmittah is in relationship ONLY to The Land of Israel. The Gematria of 911 is found and established in the very first Word of Ha Torah. Genesis 1.1 - 'In the beginning'. I see a Mystical relationship between The Firstfruits the People of Israel offered the first time 'In the beginning.'

רֵאשִׁית
Ray Sheet / Firstfruit
911 = 400 ת 10 י 300 ש 1 א 200 ר

רֵאשִׁית
Ray Sheet / first beginning
911 = 400 ת 10 י 300 ש 1 א 200 ר

We know that The People of Israel had to possess The Holy Land before they could offer firstfruits. The Gematria for הוֹרַשְׁתָּ meaning to possess is 911.

הוֹרַשְׁתָּ
Hoh Rah Shi Taw / To Possess
911 = 400 ת 300 ש 200 ר 6 ו 5 ה

Dear Ones, We have journeyed through some Mitzvot of The Torah. We have discussed, in brief, Eleven Mitzvot of The Torah. We have mystically linked Time with Gematria.

Parshat Devarim Ki Teitzei
Deuteronomy 21.10 - 25.19

Chapter Six
Unique Mentions Of Time In The Torah

Dear Ones, This week in our Parshat, references to time are unique in this instance. Words that we commonly associate with Time like day, week, month and year are not frequently used. Instead, Time is mentioned in other ways. For example Deuteronomy 21.11.

Deuteronomy 21.10 - 11
When you go forth to war against your enemies, and The Lord, your God, Has Delivered them into your hands, and you have taken them captive, and you see among the captives a beautiful woman, and desire to have her as your wife; then you shall bring her home to your house. And she shall shave her head, and pare everything from Aleph to Tav of her nails. And she must discard her prison garb from upon her. And shall remain in your house, and bewail everything from Aleph to

Tav of her father and everything from Aleph to Tav of her mother for A Month of Days. And after that you shall go into her, and be her husband, and she shall be your wife.

'When you go forth to war against your enemies' Speaks of the time that we don't know specifically. The Time is not defined like The Sabbath or The High Holy Days. This Time is defined by The Words 'when you go forth to war against your enemies.' The Time that The Torah is speaking about does not begin until specifically then. This is one of those unique times that we are discussing in this weeks Parshat.

There is a second part to Time in this Scripture. It is 'after The Lord your God Has Delivered our enemies into our hands.' The first Time is as we go to war. The second Time is after we were successful in the war, and our enemies are defeated. The third Time is when we take them captive. The fourth Time is when we see a beautiful woman and desire her as a wife. The fifth Time is when one brings this beautiful captive woman to one's home, and she shaves her head until she's completely bald. Then she pares her nails. Then she changes garments. She removes her garments of captivity. The sixth time is the 30 days of mourning for her mother and father. After all six of these times are completed, and then at that point the seventh time begins. The man that desired her can marry her. The Torah mentions seven different times with only one direct reference to a time, i.e. '*A Month of Days.*'

A portion of our discussion regarding '*A Month of Days*' must form around the words אֵשֶׁת יְפַת־תֹּאַר Ay Shet - Yih Paht - Toh Ahr - meaning A Woman who is beautiful, who is of appropriate form. Another meaning may also be 'a beautiful woman who is shapely apportioned'. Those that believe this is the correct interpretation suggest The Torah is trying to bring the soldier to his senses by having this beautiful woman mourn for her Father and Mother in his home for 30 days and by having her shave her head and cut her nails. The intent, they say is to make this beautiful woman appear unattractive and unappealing. Rabbi Nosson Scherman, The Stone Edition The Chumash (Mesorah Publications, Ltd., Brooklyn, N.Y. 1993), p. 1046

I feel that the first definition is accurate For several reasons. The only place in The Torah that the Words יֶרַח יָמִים Yeh Tah Ach Yaw Meem / A Month of Days appear is in Deuteronomy 21.13. Therefore, we recognize these words carry a special meaning and intention. Our duty is to understand the intention.

We must look behind the scenes to see what's there. When The Torah Says, '*A Month of Days*' It may appear like this is in reference to any month in the lunar cycle of either 29 or 30 days. However, our Sages Teach this is specifically in reference to The Month of Elul. During the month of Elul, we blow the shofar each day except for Shabbat. When the month of the Elul concludes, we celebrate Rosh Hashanah, The Day of the Shofar blowing, the day of judgment and the birthday of the world.

Rabbi Menachem M. Schneerson, Torah Chumash Devarim Kehot Publication Society (Brooklyn, NY 2011) p 125

Normally one begins mourning on the day of death. However, here it appears to be different. The Words יֶרַח יָמִים Yeh Tah Ach Yaw Meem / A Month of Days may be interpreted as 'A Moon of Days'. Also, we need to keep in mind that the captive woman is not Jewish. Therefore, she will need to convert before the soldier can marry her. No matter how much the soldier desires her, he may not force her to convert. The Beautiful woman must choose to convert to Judaism on her own.

The conversion process for the beautiful woman requires about a year. The beautiful woman must be taught all 613 Mitzvot of The Torah. She must understand. She must except them and practice them.

Rabbi Ellie Monk writes in <u>The Call Of The Torah</u> that the soldier is Spiritually perceptive. He is not lustful! He sees a beautiful woman.

What is it that he sees? He sees the soul of this beautiful woman. She is beautiful because of her spiritual relationship to the Lord. Therefore, he takes her to provide her soul the opportunity to observe all 613 mitzvot of The Torah as a convert. He takes a position formed by Ohr HaChaim and other Kabbalists. Rabbi Eli Munk, Call of The Torah, The Artscroll Mesorah Series, (Brooklyn, New York: Mesorah Publications, Ltd. 3rd Impression, 1994), pp 215 - 216

The Torah requires that the beautiful woman cut her hair. This is symbolic of removing her former intellect. As she learns The Torah and her hair begins to grow again she takes on a new intellect of one that is Torah observant.

The Torah requires that the beautiful woman cut her nails. This is symbolic of removing superfluous emotional indulgences. Rabbi Menachem M. Schneerson, Torah Chumash Devarim Kehot Publication Society (Brooklyn, NY 2011) p 125 also cutting one's nails is in preparation for the Mikvah Conversion. Why?

The entire body must be entirely immersed in a fresh flowing body of water. This is symbolic of cleansing oneself of the past.

Mystically there is a connection between 'A Month of Days' and dwelling. Remember how our discussion began. 'When you go to war against your enemies.' The beautiful woman is from among the enemies of The Lord God and The People of Israel. The soldier has taken his enemy captive. Normally enemies of war are in prison camps. So why does The Torah say 'You will bring her into your home?.' We teach our home is a sacred place where Torah Sayings are taught. Wouldn't this perhaps be disruptive to the home atmosphere and the learning of The Torah? One can not tolerate disruptive behavior in their home especially during the month Elul! So we know there has to be more to what The Torah is Saying. I believe The Torah is informing us that the soldier has removed this beautiful lady from the negative and harmful environment and in turn has placed her in an environment of Spirituality and Torah Observances. In other words, she used to dwell in a bad environment and now she dwells in A Torah Observant environment. This dwelling is for '*A Moon of Days*' or '*A Month of Days*.' Often when the Word יָמִים Yah Meem is used this reference is to a year. Remember in Chapter One where we discussed יָמִים Yah Meem in Deuteronomy 1.46 and 2.1?

We know conversion requires at least a year. We also know that יָמִים Yah Meem is used in reference to Years. The righteous soldier takes the beautiful woman to his home to learn and Observe Torah for a year. During this time, she is dwelling in his home. However, the intent is that she is dwelling in The Torah learning and Observance.

יֶרַח יָמִים
Yeh Tah Ach Yaw Meem / A Month of Days
318 = 40 ם 10 י 40 מ 10 י 8 ח 200 ר 10 י

יוֹשֵׁב
Yoh Shayv / To Dwell
318 = 2 ב 300 שׁ 6 ו 10 י
Remember, the normal time for mourning is

Seven Days. When the Torah Says, יָמִים Yah Meem '*A Moon of Days*' or '*A Month of Days*', We understand there is an intended meaning that we must search for. It is clear! This is not the normal type of mourning. This is a different type of mourning. As noted earlier, the period for mourning her father and her mother in this situation is during The Month of Elul. The beautiful woman has concluded her year of Torah learning and is preparing to convert. The last stage of her preparation is to mourn the Month of Elul for her father and her mother. Then on the eve of the birthday of the world, on the day of Judgment, on The Day of Remembering and on the day we blow the shofar the beautiful woman completes her conversion by going to the mikvah and immerses herself, thus completing the conversion process. She is now available to her husband on the Day of remembering.

What does The Torah Say about Sarah, Rachel, and Hannah? 'On The New Year Sarah, Rachel and Hannah were visited,' i.e. they conceived.' Think about what this means. Rosh Hashanah is this incredibly Holy Day. Rosh Hashanah is also a date for physical relations with one's spouse. It is on this day that the soldier and the beautiful woman consummate their marriage.

Deuteronomy 21.18 - 21
If a man has a stubborn and rebellious son, who will not obey the voice of his father, or the voice of his mother, and who, when they have chastened him, will not listen to them. Then shall his father and his mother lay hold of him and bring him out to the elders of his city, and to the gate of his place. And they shall say to the elders of his city, 'This our son, is stubborn and rebellious. He will not obey our voice. He is a glutton and a drunkard.' And all the men of his city shall stone him with stones that he dies; so shall you put evil away from among you; and all Israel shall hear, and fear.

We have another example of Time not being mentioned in verses 18 through 21. The first mention of Time is '*if a man has a stubborn son.*' The second dimension of Time is '*if a man has a rebellious son.*' The Third mention of Time is when the son refuses to '*obey the voice of his father*'. The fourth mention of Time is when the son refuses to '*obey the voice of his mother.*'

Somewhere in the midst of these Times are two other Times. There are the Times when the son is gluttonous. There is the Time when the son is a drunkard. How many Times does it take For one to be gluttonous? How many Times does it take for one to be a drunkard? These Times are evident, but we cannot say how many Times each represents.

The next dimension of Time is when each of these Times has been repeated multiple Times. Then the next Time is when the father and the mother take hold of their son and bring him to the elders of the city at the gate place. There has to be a determination. The son has to be found guilty. There have to be witnesses. Finally, After all of these Times are completed The final Time comes where the son is stoned to death, and he dies.

Deuteronomy 21.22 - 23

And if a man has committed a sin deserving death, and he is to be put to death, and you hang him on a tree; His body shall not remain all night upon the tree, but you shall bury him that day; for he who is hanged is accursed by God; that your land, which The Lord your God Gives you for an inheritance, be not defiled.

At the conclusion of Chapter 21, Scripture speaks of a Time when a man has committed a capital offense that deserves death. Then Scripture Speaks of the Time after he has been put to death. Scripture is Speaking to the Time when his body is hanging on a wooden tree. There are some Times indicators. Scripture is speaking of definite Times. Scripture concludes this observance by giving us a definite reference to Time, *'you are to bury him that day.'*

Within this Parshat, there are many examples of Time Observances that don't stand out because keywords noting Times are not used. Each of these is a Time.

Deuteronomy 24.16

When you lend your brother anything, you shall not go into his house to fetch his pledge. You shall stand outside, and the man to whom you lend shall bring out the pledge outside to you. And if the man is poor, you shall not sleep in his pledge; You shall deliver him the pledge back when the sun goes down, that he may sleep in his garment, and bless you; and it shall be righteousness to you before The Lord your God.

Again, we Observe a point in Time. It is 'before the sun goes down.'

Our goal in this Chapter is to again draw our attention to different ways in which Time is related in The Holy Scriptures.

Parshat Devarim Ki Tavo
Deuteronomy 26.1 - 29.8

Lesson Seven

Time To Acknowledge We Are Blessed!

Dear Ones, We began a portion of this discussion in Chapter Five. In Chapter Five I stated, 'This is where we are at today. We are 3,287 years from when Moses spoke these Words. Today in 5776 From Creation, The Jewish people do not occupy all of The Land Promised to them by The Lord God. Millions of Jews live outside of Eretz Yisroel. The Levites do not occupy the Forty-Eight Cities as intended in Scripture. The land outside the Forty-Eight cities has been altered. I am saying the Mitzvot spoken of in the above Scriptures will need to be reestablished again as it was in the Days of Joshua! There will be a serious war to reclaim our land. Jews from every corner of the world will come to help liberate The Land of Israel again. Some countries maybe wiped off the face of the earth.

Moshiach / Messiah will come at the 'End of Days' our enemies will be defeated once and for all! I am saying The People will fight these wars again as in the days of Joshua. So as a result, it is like each of us is standing before the great Prophet Moses hearing His Words again 3,287 Years later. We return to the subject at hand.

2488 FC
Once The Land of Israel is conquered, Jewish farmers will settle The land and plant crops of grain, i.e. wheat, oats, rye, barley and spelt. Then at a period in Time after these Times they will harvest their First Fruit.'

In this week's Parshat, we learn about rejoicing because of all the good The Lord God Has Given to us.

Devarim 26.11

וְשָׂמַחְתָּ בְכָל־הַטּוֹב אֲשֶׁר נָתַן־לְךָ יְהֹוָה אֱלֹהֶיךָ וּלְבֵיתֶךָ אַתָּה וְהַלֵּוִי וְהַגֵּר אֲשֶׁר בְּקִרְבֶּךָ׃

Deuteronomy 26.11
You shall rejoice with all the good that The Lord your God Gave you, and your household, and the Levi, and the proselyte in your midst.

All the good is the Gematria of 74. Eternity is also the Gematria 74. Let's note the unique connection between Time and Gematria here. Also, we should note the importance of Observing ALL 613 Mitzvot of The Torah. In this Parshat, we learn of the Blessings and curses. We notice the last of the curses in Deuteronomy 27.26.

Devarim 27.26
אָר֗וּר אֲשֶׁ֧ר לֹא־יָקִ֛ים אֶת־דִּבְרֵ֥י הַתּוֹרָֽה־הַזֹּ֖את לַעֲשׂ֣וֹת אוֹתָ֑ם וְאָמַ֥ר כָּל־הָעָ֖ם אָמֵֽן׃

Deuteronomy 27.26
Cursed is the one that does not stand up for everything from Aleph to Tav of The Words of This, The Torah to perform Them and all The People said, 'Amen!.

When One of The People of Israel do not Observe a Mitzvot of The Torah, this is a point in Time when that one is cursed. Why am I pointing this out? It is because **every Observance of The Torah is important.** Well-meaning individuals attempt to persuade The People of Israel that the Observances in The Torah are fulfilled and that we no longer need to Observe them. They mean well but they are mistaken!

We are The Holy People because we have responsibilities requiring us to Observe The 613 Commands of The Torah. Observing the 613 Commands separates The People of Israel from the rest of the world. The Holy Scripture is informing us that we have a choice to be blessed or to be cursed. No one wants to be cursed! When we, The People of Israel fail to Observe The 613 Commands of The Torah that The Lord God Requires of us, we cannot be the blessing to the families of the world that The Lord God Intends us to be!! The Parshat concludes with a reminder of what is is like to be Blessed.

Deuteronomy 28.1 - 8

And it shall come to pass, if you shall diligently heed The Voice of The Lord your God by observing and doing All His Commandments which I command you this day, that the Lord your God will set you high above all nations of the earth. And all these blessings shall come on you, and overtake you if you shall listen to the voice of the Lord your God. Blessed shall you be in the city, and blessed shall you be in the field. Blessed shall be the fruit of your body, and the fruit of your ground, and the fruit of your cattle, the produce of your cows, and the flocks of your sheep. Blessed shall be your basket and your store. Blessed shall you be when you come in, and blessed shall you be when you go out. The Lord Shall Cause your enemies who rise up against you to be defeated before your face. They shall come out against you one way, and flee before you seven ways. The Lord Shall Command the blessing upon you in your storehouses, and in all that you set your hand to, and He Shall Bless You in the land that the Lord your God Gives you.

The Lord Said,

Genesis 12.2 - 3
'And I Will Make of you a great nation, and I Will Bless you, and make your name great; and you shall be a blessing; And I will bless those who bless you, and curse him who curses you; **and in you shall all families of the earth be blessed.'**

Some individuals do not understand that The Blessing for The People of Israel comes from our faithful adherence to doing what The Lord God Has Commanded. If we fail to do what The Lord Has Commanded us, we are cursed. When we Observe the 613 Commands in The Torah, we are blessed.

On one day somewhere in the last Days of Moses's life, Moses took the time to remind us of this important principle of Observing every Command of The Torah. Now, Thousands of Years Later there are many Commands in The Torah that we cannot Observe. I shared a few in Chapter Five regarding the Levites and The

Land that we can no longer Observe. This is not good!! Still, even though there are some Commands, we cannot fulfill we should do our very best to Observe The Commands that are within our reach. Honestly, This is not about how long one prays or studies The Torah each Day. It's about the sincerity of one's heart And the attitude that we possess.

Let's return us the Gematria of 74. We are to express thanks and appreciation for every good thing The Lord Gives us.

בְּכָל־הַטּוֹב
Vih Cawl - Hah Tohv / In All The Good [The Lord Has Given us]
74 = 2 ב 6 ו 9 ט 5 ה 30 ל 20 כ 2 ב

What do we say each Day in our prayers?

Psalms 145.
Remember David's Psalm of Praise?
I will extol you, my God, O King; and I will bless your Name for ever and ever. Every day I will bless you, and I will praise your name for

ever and ever. Great is The Lord, and greatly to be praised, and his greatness is unsearchable. One generation shall praise your works to another and shall declare your mighty acts. I will speak of the glorious splendor of your majesty, and of your wondrous works. And men shall speak of the might of your awesome acts, and I will declare your greatness. They shall utter the fame of your great goodness, and shall sing of your righteousness. The Lord is Gracious and full of compassion; slow to anger, and of abundant loving kindness. The Lord is good to all, and His Mercies are over all His works. All your works shall praise you, O Lord; and your pious ones shall bless you.

עַד
Ahd / Ahd Eternity
74 = 4 ד 70 ע

עֵד
Ayd / Witness
74 = 4 ד 70 ע

יִסַד
Yee Sahd / To Appoint / To set up
74 = 4 ד 60 ס 10 י

Psalms 119.89
Forever, O Lord is Your Word fixed in Heaven.

What did we read in Deuteronomy 28.1? *'And it shall come to pass if you shall give heed diligently to The Voice of The Lord your God...'*

Each Time we thank The Lord God for what He Has Given us is a Point in Time! Each of us should have many of these points in Time. We choose the appointed Time to say 'Thank you!'. We are the witnesses of His Blessings throughout eternity.

Page 146

Parshat Devarim Nitzavim
Deuteronomy 29.9 - 30.20

Lesson Eight

The End of Days

Dear Ones, within this week's Parshat there are Thirteen usages of The Word הַיּוֹם 'This Day'. We will review one.

Deuteronomy 29.9

Moses Said to The People of Israel, 'You are standing up This day, all of you before The Lord your God; your captains of your tribes, your elders, and your officers, with all the men of Israel, Your little ones, your wives, and your stranger who is in your camp, from the hewer of your wood to the drawer of your water; so that [each of] you should enter into Covenant with The Lord your God, and into His oath, which The Lord your God Makes with you This Day.'

This Day was the Day The People of Israel

were Standing before The Presence of The Lord God and His Representative, Moses, their Teacher. The Word נִצָּבִים Nee Tzaw Veem means to stand up. נִצָּבִים Nee Tzaw Veem also means to stand up for a principle. The Torah is Sharing more than a principle. The Torah Is informing us that The people of Israel were actively engaged. They stood for The Principles of The Torah. They Stood up for The Observances of The Torah. What we read goes beyond just standing up. This time and place נִצָּבִים Nee Tzaw Veem means enthusiastically standing up, enthusiastically participating and enthusiastically engaging.

נִצָּבִים Nee Tzaw Veem Is more than mental assent. צָבִים Nee Tzaw Veem is more than agreeing with what The Torah Says. צָבִים Nee Tzaw Veem describes our 100% commitment, our 100% firm engagement, and our 100% enthusiasm for The Words of The Torah, The Mitzvot, and The Covenant. At that time, The People of Israel displayed a distinct sharpness like a soldier who has intensely agonized over his preparation for dress inspection. He stands out. He looks sharp and crisp among other soldiers. The People of Israel were sharp and crisp among the nations of the world, at that time. Mystically we were in a place and time.

נִצָּבִים
Nee Tzaw Veem
To enthusiastically stand up for a principal
192 = 40מ 10י 2ב 90צ 50נ

וּמָקוֹם
Voo Mah Kohm
And [being in a certain] place
192 = 40מ 6ו 100ק 40מ 6ו

בַּפַּעַם
Bah Pah Ahm
[Being] In a specific time
192 = 40מ 70ע 80פ 2ב

Later in our discussion we will read in Ezekiel 38 how The Lord collects His People. The root Word for מְקַבֶּצֶת Mih Qu Beh Tzet meaning to gather is קבץ. The Gematria for קבץ is 192.

מְקַבֶּצֶת
קַבֵּץ
Kah Baytz / To Gather - To Collect
192 = 90ץ 2ב 100ק

Mystically we make this link where we, The People of Israel were before The Lord God at a specific place and at a specific time. We appeared distinct and sharp. We stood up enthusiastically for The Torah, The Mitzvot, and The Covenant. This is where we were. This is where we need to be!!

Where are we today? Let's move a little further into our Parshat To another day and time when our heart turned away from the Lord God. Unfortunately for us, we strayed from The Mitzvot of The Torah. We served gods of other nations. The words of The Curse came upon us. We were stubbornly drunk with our business and our self-importance. Our sins caused us to be scattered among the nations of the world. Our land was desolate after all the punishments come upon us. We lost our sharpness. We were no longer crisp. We no longer enthusatically stood up for The Observances of The Torah.

Eventually, we will come back to our Spiritual senses. We will return to The Lord and again enthusiastically stand up for The Torah, The Mitzvot, and The Covenant. We will Observe The Mitzvot of The Torah! At that Place and at that time when we obey all that The Lord Commanded us On 'This Day,' i.e. the Day that Moses Spoke to us.

Our failings point to The End of Days that our Father Jacob spoke of in Genesis 49.1

Genesis 49.1
And Jacob called to his sons, and said, Gather yourselves together, that I may tell you that which shall befall you at The End of Days.

Do we understand what Jacob spoke of when He used the term End of Days? Please notice the date September 9, 2015, in The 2016 Bible Journeys Calendar. Do we understand what happened on this day? Do we know what this Day represents? Astute readers may say, 'This

Day was the first day God began His Creating of the universe.' They would be correct. However, This Day is more than just the First Day of The Lord God's Creating. There were Six days of creation. Five days of creating were during The Last Days of the Twelveth Month Of The Original Calendar. These Five days were prior to The Lord God resting. In The Jewish Calendar, they are from Elul 25 – 29.

Let's return to The 2016 Bible Journeys Calendar. Notice the six Days of Creating. Day Six in 2015 is a Monday. Originally Day Six was a Friday. The Sixth Day of Creating is not part of The Last Days. Day Six is The Day of Judgment that we read about in Genesis Three.

On The Sixth Day we are Taught Adam's dust was gathered from the location in front of The Holy Altar of The Holy Temple in Jerusalem. The Holy Dust was kneaded into a shapeless mass. In The Third Hour, Adams limbs were shaped. In The Fourth Hour, The Lord God 'Breathed into his nostrils the breath of life; and Adam became a living soul'. In The Fifth

Hour, Adam arose and stood on his feet. In The Sixth Hour, Adam Gave Names to all the Animals. In The Seventh Hour, Eve was separated from Adam. In The Eighth Hour, Eve became his Wife. They consummated their relationship. Cain and his twin sister were born. In Ninth Hour Adam and Eve were Instructed In The Seven Laws all humans are to Observe. The universe functions according to These Observances. In The Tenth Hour Adam and Eve sinned. In The Eleventh, Adam and Eve were Tried and Judged. In The Twelfth Hour before the sunset and Sabbath began in Gan Eden / The Garden of Eden Adam and Eve were expelled. Sabbath 38b

The point is on The Day of Judgment humankind departed The Garden of Eden. The Prophet Isaiah Prophesied that on this same Day, i.e. The Day of Judgment, the outcasts among Israel will be gathered back.

Isaiah 27.13
And it shall come to pass on that Day, that the great shofar shall be blown, and those shall

come who were lost in the land of Assyria, and the outcasts in the land of Egypt, and shall worship The Lord on the Holy Mount at Jerusalem.

This immediately follows the Shmittah Year. Our Rabbis Teach that the end of the Seven Year Cycle The Son of David, i.e. Messiah will come on The First Day of The First Year of the New Seven Year Cycle. Sanhedrin 97a

This will be The Year of Jubilee when The Land is Returned, all prior debt is forgiven, and all slaves are released among The People of Israel.

Our Parshat Speaks of This Day in Deuteronomy 30.1 – 7. Verse Five begins with The Word וֶהֱבִיאֲךָ Veh Heh Vee Ah Kaw meaning 'to bring.' Please make a note of this because we will return to this point when we discuss Moses prophecy later. Why? The Gematria points to The Jubilee Year.

Devarim 30.1 - 7

'And it shall come to pass, when all these things have come upon you, the blessing and the curse, which I have set before you, and you shall call them to mind among all the nations, where the Lord your God has driven you, And shall return to the Lord your God, and shall obey his voice according to all that I command you this day, you and your children, with all your heart, and with all your soul; That then the Lord your God will turn your captivity, and have compassion upon you, and will return and gather you from all the nations, where the Lord your God has scattered you. If your outcasts have been driven out to the farthest parts of heaven, from there will the Lord your God gather you, and from there will he fetch you; And the Lord, your God, will bring you into the land that your fathers possessed, and you shall possess it; and he will do you good, and multiply you above your fathers. And the Lord your God will circumcise your heart, and the heart of your seed, to love the Lord your God with all your heart, and with all your soul, that you may live. And the Lord your God will

put all these curses upon your enemies, and on those who hate you, who persecuted you.'

Some Teach that we do not know the Day or The Hour Messiah will come/ This is not entirely true. There are pointers that offer some direction.

We know Messiah will come immediately following The Last Days. The last Days are 25 Elul through 29 Elul. The Last Days are the last days of the old year. Rosh HaShanah begins the New Year. The shofar is blown on Rosh HaShanah.

We know that Messiah will come immediately after the Last Days of the week. The Last Days of The Week Are Friday and Sabbath. The Lord God is precise.

Genesis 2.2 – 3
And on the Seventh Day God Ended His work that He Had Made, and He Rested on The Seventh Day from all His work that He Had Made. And God Blessed The Seventh Day, and

Sanctified It; because that in it, He Had rested from all his work which God Created and Made.

We know The Messiah will come on Sabbath Rosh Ha Shannah immediately following the Shmittah Year. Sanhedrin 97a Some believe Messiah will come following the Seventh Seven Year Cycle, i.e. the 49th Year. [7 Years x 7 Years] - Some think The Messiah will come in the Fiftieth Year. Some believe the Fiftieth Year is the Year of Jubilee.

It is on This Day, i.e. Rosh Ha Shanah that we, The People of Israel gather to weep and seek repentance for our sins. The Lord God will see our sincerity. The Lord God will be Moved to gather us to The Land of Israel.

We know The Messiah will come in The Last Days of The Last Of The Years according to Ezekiel 38.

Ezekiel 38.8
After many Days, you will have paid for [past

sins], at The End of The Years you will come to The Land that is restored from the destruction. You will be gathered from among many nations, [By The Lord] to The Mountains of Israel that were continually desolate [of people]. And He will bring you forth from nations, and you shall dwell securely with them [your people].

Dear Ones The People of Israel do not posses all of The Holy Land The Lord God Gave to us. How will The People of Israel gain ownership and full control of every meter of The Land of Israel? Possessing all The Holy Land will require a huge miracle. Today we are capable of receiving minute by minute information as it unfolds in our world. We know the present Day picture in The Holy Land of Israel looks gruesome. It looks like war is coming. There are disputes as to who owns all The Holy Land of Israel. These disputes must be settled! They will be settled!

Moses Prophesied!
Deuteronomy 30.5
'The Lord your God Will Bring you into [The

Holy Land Of Israel] which your fathers possessed, and you will possess The Holy Land Of Israel; The Lord, your God, Will do good for you, and multiply you above your fathers.'

We know Deuteronomy 30.5 is a prophesy for our present age because of the Words הָאָרֶץ אֲשֶׁר־יָרְשׁוּ אֲבֹתֶיךָ.

The Word אֲבֹתֶיךָ Ah Voh Teh Caw means 'Your Fathers'. Deuteronomy 30.5 informs us that after Joshua and The Army of Israel conquered all The Holy Land, then partitoned The Holy Land to each Tribe, then possessed The Holy Land, and after our sins we were displaced from The Holy Land of Israel, and we were scattered to the four corners of the earth. It is from the four corners of The Earth that The Lord God Will bring each of us back to The Holy Land.

Today more of The People of Israel live outside of The Holy Land than those living in The Holy Land.
- The Lord God has not brought all of us To

The Holy Land of Israel yet.

- The People of Israel do not possess all The Holy Land of Israel that our Fathers possessed. Today The People of Israel possess a portion of The Holy Land, so this portion of the prophecy remains to be fulfilled. The People of Israel must possess the entire Holy Land including all of the Holy City, Jerusalem. Moses prophesied, ' You will possess The Land.'

The birth of Isaac was to give Abraham a son to inherit and to possess The Land of Canaan. The Gematria of יָרְשׁוּ Yaw Rih Shoo meaning to possess is the Gematria 516. The Gematria of יוֹרֵשׁ Yoh Raysh meaning to inherit is also the Gematria 516.

In Chapter Five we discussed The Mitzvot that require us to both possess all The Holy Land of Israel and to inherit all The Holy Land of Israel. In Chapter Five I stated there are some Mitzvot that cannot be Observed until The People of Israel possess all of the Holy Land. What does this mean?

Dear Reader, Deuteronomy 30.5 remains to be entirely fulfilled.

Dear Reader the clock is ticking until The Lord God Brings The People of Israel back into complete possession of The Land of Israel. What conditions MUST exist for The People of Israel to Possess all the Land of Israel?

Questions arise with regards to Jeremiah 33.

Jeremiah 33.12 - 18
Thus says The Lord of Hosts; Again in this place, which is desolate without man and without beast, and in all its cities, shall be a habitation of shepherds who make their flocks lie down. In the cities of the mountains, in the cities of the Shephelah, and in the cities of the Negev, and in the land of Benjamin, and in the places around Jerusalem, and in the cities of Judah, shall the flocks pass again under the hands of him who tells them, Says The Lord. Behold, The Days come, Says The Lord, that I will perform that good thing that I have promised to the house of Israel and the house

of Judah. In those Days, and at that Time, I will cause an offshoot of righteousness to grow up from David; and he shall execute judgment and righteousness in The Land. In those Days, Judah shall be saved, and Jerusalem shall dwell safely; and this is the name by which she shall be called, 'The Lord is our Righteousness.' For thus Says The Lord; David shall never lack a man to sit upon the throne of the house of Israel; Neither shall The Priests, or The Levites lack a man before me to offer burnt offerings, and to kindle Meal Offerings, and to do sacrifice continually.

The 'Again' in Verse Twelve is implied. Is this about two destructions of The Land of Israel? Some Rabbis were opposed to Israel becoming a nation in 1948. Why? Because, in their opinion The Lord did not do this. If they are correct, is there the possibility of another destruction? Those in control of The Holy Land must return The Holy Land to the tribes of original inheritance BEFORE The Year of Jubilee. In Joshua's Day, The Holy Land was taken little by little through the war at The

Lord God's Direction. Perhaps this will be the course again. . . Then perhaps a second destruction awaits.

The People of Israel are in The Time of Blessing and the Time of Curse. Many of The People of Israel fulfill the Observances they can but cannot fulfill them all. This is the curse. We are stuck. The great Sage, Rambam cautions us to be careful about attempting to pinpoint the prophetic dates. Rabbi Nosson Scherman, The Stone Edition Tanach (Mesorah Publications, Ltd., Brooklyn, N.Y. 1993), p. 351Second Edition p 1299.

There is a process. I mentioned we have points in time that help us determine when The Last Days are upon us. I don't see the events happening in our present age aligning perfectly with The Prophesies written in The Holy Scriptures at this time. 5776 From Creation. This could change quickly! To possess The Holy Land means Time will be required to acquire ever meter of The Holy Land again. Time will be required to divide between Tribes.

Time will be required to determine which Tribe each of us is a descendant. Then the Tribal Leaders must settle descendants into their Land. Then after each of us are settled in our Land. It is then that each of us possess The Land. Then we can again begin celebrating the Year of Jubilee in The Holy Land Of Israel.

By some accounts, this year we are in the seventh year of the seven Shmittah years. We are in the 49th year, i.e. the Year of Jubilee right now, i.e. this Year. By other accounts, the Year of Jubilee will begin on Rosh HaShanah 5776 and conclude on Yom Kipper of 5777 FC From Creation at nightfall.

If, in the very near future, the Bet Din were to declare this to be the Year of Jubilee according to one of the above calculations Great miracles beyond our imagination would be required. The Bet Din cannot proclaim a true Year of Jubilee until The People of Israel are completely in possession of The Holy Land. In The Year of Jubilee, The Holy Land must be returned to the Tribe from which it inherited it.

וֶהֱבִיאֲךָ Heh Vee Ah Kaw meaning 'to bring' in Deuteronomy 30.5 is the Gematria of 44. The Word Jubilee is also the Gematria of 44.

וֶהֱבִיאֲךָ
Veh Heh Vee Ah Kaw / And To Bring
44 = 20ך 1א 10י 2ב 5ה 6ו

בַּיֹּבֵל
Bah Yoh Vayl / In Jubilee
44 = 30ל 2ב 10י 2ב

לְבָבִי
Lih Vaw Vee / My Heart
44 = 10י 2ב 2ב 30ל

What is the Mystical meaning? The Lord God Brings The People of Israel to The Holy Land to possess The Land so we can return to Observing all Mitzvot, especially The Year of Jubilee.

Part of the process, i.e. one of the points in time is when The People of Israel are brought to The Holy Land, The Lord God Will

Circumcise our heart.

This is a discussion about Time and Gematria. At this Time, The People of Israel are still living in the Time of Blessing and curse. The curse is that we are not Observing all 613 Commands of The Torah. Many of us live outside The Land, Our hearts are not circumcised. We do not possess all The Land. We cannot pass The Land on to our children as an inheritance. The Third Temple must be built. Articles of The Holy Temple must be restored. The Priests and Levites must be dedicated and assigned to their positions.

Messiah must come. There is the war that must be fought. The enemies of Israel must be defeated. Children must be born in Israel thus showing security. We must multiply. Then, when all is aligned in the order that The Lord God Intends, we will do Good. We will be the Blessing spoken of in Genesis Twelve.

Vayeilech
Deuteronomy 31.1 - 30

Chapter Nine

Time of Rebellion at The End of Days

Dear Ones, In this Weeks Parshat, our Teacher Moses shares about rebellion. How serious is the rebellion among The People of Israel, among us today?

Deuteronomy 21.27
Moses Said, 'For I know everything from Aleph to Tav of 'Meh Rih Yih Caw' your rebelliousness and your stiff neck. Behold! While I am still alive with you this day, you have been rebellious against the Lord; and how much more after my death!'

כִּי אָנֹכִי יָדַעְתִּי אֶת־מֶרְיְךָ

'For I know everything from Aleph to Tav of Meh Rih Yih Caw' your rebelliousness. . .' Who is Moses speaking of? Is Moses speaking of The People of Israel in 2488 From Creation? Is

He speaking about The People of Israel in our age? Is he speaking of both?

מֶרְיְךָ
'Meh Rih Yih Caw' means 'your rebellion'.
270 = 20 ךְ 10 יְ 200 ר 40 מֶ

The Gematria of מֶרְיְךָ Meh Rih Yih Caw your rebelliousness is 270. What does this represent?

Dear Friends, this Parshat is often studied during The Ten Days of Repentance. We should be examining ourselves. We should be considering every possibility of sin. What did the Lord Say about the Generation that was destroyed in the flood?

Genesis 6.5
And God Saw that the wickedness of man was great in the earth and that every imagination of the thoughts of his heart was only evil continually.

רַע כָּל־הַיּוֹם Evil All the Day. רַע Rah means evil.

The Gematria of Rah is also 270.

רַע
Rah / Evil
270 = 70 ע 200 ר

We can Mystically see how rebellion and evil travel on the same paths.

Dear Reader, the issue with many of us is we were raised in life styles where Torah Observance was not prevalent. Our lives were not filled with Words of The Torah. Our lives were not surrounded by Torah living. Unfortunately, living a life outside of total Torah Observance maybe be common for us. Living a Torah Observant life maybe seem abnormal?

As I share what should be abnormal for us it is with a caveat; I was also raised estranged to The 613 Observances of The Torah. At that time, the Observances of The Torah were strange to me. My choice of clothing was outrageous. I did not dress as a man with virtue. My choice of clothing was not moral. I did not dress like an individual with high moral standards. I did not use language representing Torah Values. There were many abnormalities with the way I lived in comparison to living a Torah Observant life. Unfortunately, my abnormalities were the norm. This is the way it is for some. We must work to reconstruct our life.

It may not be our intention to live in rebellion to The Observances of The Torah. We may not be aware of the each Torah Observance. We may not understand the importance of us living a Torah life. Whatever the reason is for us to live abnormally, i.,e in rebellion to The Torah, we need to stop. We need to seek help in reconstructing our life!! The world depends on us to Observe The Mitzvot of The Torah. The world needs the blessings our Torah Observant life will bring.

Today, decades later my past life has slowly become strange. Thank God!

Many of us are somewhere in-between how I used to live and how I now live. It is important for us to work on ourselves. We must work on our middot - our character traits as well as our Observance. We must be the best that we can be!!

What is the point? Some of us need to back up a little. We should consider if we are estranged to The Torah as I was. The Word נֵכָר Nah Cawr means 'Strange'. The Gematria for נֵכָר Nah Cawr is 270.

נֵכָר
Nah Cawr / Strange
270 = 200 ר 20 כ 50 נ

The point is this. Perhaps we are estranged to The Observances of The Torah because of how we were raised before we began our return to The Lord God. Are we rebellious? Are some of our actions rebellious? Maybe! Do we guard how we speak? Is our choice of clothing modest? How do we conduct our lives? What does guarding the Sabbath mean to us? Does guarding The Sabbath have meaning for us? Do we show loving-kindness to everyone?

Dear Ones, we are in the midst of the Ten Days of Repentance for the Year 5776 From Creation. So studying Vayeilech is appropriate. Why is studying Vayeilech appropriate? Moses speaks to us, The People of Israel as a Prophet. That very day he perceived rebellion among the hearts of The People of Israel. Moses was speaking to each of us. What Moses said might be difficult to except. Yet, We know Moses had the clearest perception of any prophet. We know Moses was right. Still, it is difficult to accept. What is rebellion?

Rebelliousness is showing a desire to resist authority, control, or convention:

Disobedience is failure or refusal to obey rules or someone in authority:

Mutiny is an open rebellion against the proper authorities.

Insurgence is rising in active revolt:

Insubordination is defiance of authority; refusal to obey orders

Do any of these Words describe us? Do any of these words describe how we may act from time to time? If so, we know that is not good.

Verse Twenty-Seven causes me a great deal of concern. I am troubled! In Chapter Eight we discussed the end of times. In this Parshat, we are knocking on the door again. Verse Twenty-Nine Discusses our Spiritual condition at The End of Days. It is up to us to reconstruct out lives in a positive way.

Moses Said, Evil will befall you at The End of Days? We do not want evil to come upon us. We do not want evil to befall us. We can take positive actions to redirect our course.

Deuteronomy 31.29
For I know that after my death you will completely corrupt yourselves, and turn aside

from the way that I have commanded you; and evil will befall you at the End of Days because you will do evil in the sight of The Lord, to provoke Him to anger through the work of your hands.

Are we living in this Time? Perhaps. Are some of us are provoking The Lord? Has The Lord Turned away from us? Should we be asking, 'How long Oh Lord Will You Turn away from your people?'

We should be examining how we are living.

What do you think?

Ha'azinu
Deuteronomy 32.1 - 52

Lesson Ten

A Time of Justice And Security At The End of Days

Dear Ones,

In the previous Chapter, we discussed A Time of Rebellion at The End of Days. Parshat Vayeilech concluded with These Words:

Deuteronomy 31.27 - 30
For I know your rebellion, and your stiff neck; behold, while I am still alive with you this day, you have been rebellious against the Lord; and how much more after my death! Gather to me all the elders of your tribes, and your officers, that I may speak these words in their ears, and call heaven and earth to witness against them. For I know that after my death you will completely corrupt yourselves, and turn aside from the way that I have commanded you; and

evil will befall you in the latter days; because you will do evil in the sight of the Lord, to provoke him to anger through the work of your hands. And Moses spoke in the ears of all the congregation of Israel the words of this poem until they were ended.

We are informed in Ha'azinu that The People of Israel will be judged for being rebellious.

Devarim 32.36

כִּי־יָדִין יְהֹוָה עַמּוֹ וְעַל־עֲבָדָיו יִתְנֶחָם כִּי יִרְאֶה כִּי־אָזְלַת יָד וְאֶפֶס עָצוּר וְעָזוּב:

Deuteronomy 32.36
For The Lord Shall Render Justice for His People, and later He will [out of Kindness] Reconsider his servants, when He Sees the power of [their enemies] surging, and none [of His People] are structured or fortified.

Notice the Second Word יָדִין Yaw Deen meaning Judgment or Justice. The root Word is דִין Deen meaning to Judge. However, we notice that an extra Letter is added to the beginning of The Word דִין Deen. The Letter י Yod is added to The Word דִין Deen. Why is this? What is the purpose for adding and extra י Yod?

The Letter י Yod is One of The Letters in The Holy Name of The Lord. Adding The Letter י Yod brings strength to an already strong Word. The Letter י Yod adds both strength and harmony. Rabbi Michael Munk The Wisdom In The Hebrew Alphabet Mesorah Publications, Brooklyn, N.Y. 1990), p. 131. The Letter י Yod is the smallest of all The Hebrew Aleph Bet. The Yod is small like a dot. The Letter י Yod represents the power of creating. The Talmud Relates that The Lord Used The Letters of His Name Yaw ה י to Create this world and the World to come. 'This world was created with The Letter ה Hey and the future world was created with The Letter י Yod.'

The left leg of The Letter ה Hey is suspended. The left leg is not connected to the rest of The Letter. Notice the opening at the Top of The

Letter ה Hey. The opening is an entrance for those desiring to repent. When we sin... When we rebel, it is like we leave the path. The opening at the top of The Letter ה Hey allows us to rejoin The Path. Menachos 29b

The Letter Yod appears Twice Within the First Seven Words of The Torah, Genesis 1.1. The Yod appears in The Word בְּרֵאשִׁית 'In the beginning and The Word הַשָּׁמַיִם The Heavens.' The Yod also appears in The Word צַדִּיק Righteous. We see a common thread. It takes strength to be a righteous person.

We are taught that our world exists because of the Lamed-Vav Tzadikim, i.e. Thirty-Six Righteous people in each generation. Abaye Said: 'The world must contain not less than Thirty-Six Righteous men in each generation who are granted sight of The Shechinah's Countenance. Isaiah Wrote, 'Blessed are all they that לוֹ 'wait' for him. The numerical value of לוֹ 'loh / wait' is Thirty-Six. Sanhedrin 97b and Sukkah 45b.

לוֹ
Loh / To Wait
לֹ 30 ו 6= 36

Bereisheit 1.1
בְּרֵאשִׁית בָּרָא אֱלֹהִים אֵת הַשָּׁמַיִם וְאֵת הָאָרֶץ:

We see the ׳ Yod being connected to The Lord, to creating, to The Heavens and to The Righteous. The Heavens are where the Righteous go to reside. Is It, for this reason, the future world was created with the Letter ׳ Yod? It is because there are only a few righteous men in the world to come.

As noted before The Word דִין Deen has an extra ׳ Yod added. The Second ׳ Yod represents extra strength, extra emphasis in Justice and Righteousness. David informs us that 'The Judgments of The Lord are True and Righteous altogether,' Psalms 19.10.

Deuteronomy 32 informs us that the Lord Shall Render Justice for His People. Later, because of His Lovingkindness He will Reconsider His servants, when He Sees the power of [their enemies] surging, and none [of The People of Israel] is structured or fortified. It is then, at The End of Days The Lord God will bring Justice for The Land of Israel and The People of Israel. This is why there is a Second Yod. Justice must be balanced. On Rosh HaShanah, The Lord issues his Judgment. On Yom Kippur, He shows benevolence to His Servants.

יָדִין
Yaw Deen / Justice
74 = 50 ן 10 י 4 ד 10 י

י ד ן
Look how different Yaw Deen is when spaces are placed between the two Yuds and the following Letter. The יד represents power. יּן are the first Two Letters of ינה meaning to oppress to trample down.

Deuteronomy 32.15 - 26 Speaks of the failings of The People of Israel. We have a long history of failing The Lord. Each Yom Kippur we keep coming to The Lord with our failings without improving. The insincere repentance of some of us becomes old. We are going through the motions. There is a short period where The Lord God of Israel turns His Face away from His People. This Yud of Justice is represented by The Yud in דִין Deen. Between Rosh Ha Shannah and Yom Kippur are Ten Days. The Letter Yud is the Gematria of Ten. Moshiach Ben Yoseif comes to lead the armies of Israel. He is defeated and killed. All hope seems gone for The People of Israel. However on Yom Kippur Moshiach Ben David comes after The Lord Brings Justice on the enemies of His People and Justice to The Land of Israel.

This justice is for oppressing The people of Israel and The Land of Israel. This Justice is for trampling on The People of Israel and The Land of Israel!

Deuteronomy 32.27 begins a Second Yud of Justice.

Our Sages Teach that the Nations of the world plan to exceed reasonable punishment for The

People of Israel. The Leaders of these countries intention is to successfully wiped Israel off the face of the earth. The Lord God Will not permit this. The enemy nations will not understand why One from the Army of Israel can no longer pursue a Thousand or why Two from the Army of Israel can no longer pursue and defeat Ten Thousand. They will claim Israel's ruin was do to their strength. If the pursuit were changed, and One Thousand from the Army of Israel were to flee before One of their enemies, and Ten Thousand of the Army of Israel were to flee before two of their enemies, the conquering nations would not understand! If this were to happen their success would ONLY be due to The Lord God turning away from His People. The enemy nations would not acknowledge God's Hand in their victory. The enemy nations would take all the credit for defeating the armies of Israel. Moses Prophesies, The Lord God Will not permit this to happen. Rabbi Menachem M. Schneerson, Torah Chumash Shemot Kehot Publication Society (Brooklyn, NY 2006) pp 199 - 207

The Prophet Ezekiel 39 Speaks of The Lord's Judgment and destruction of the enemy nations. Seven months will be required to bury all the dead. Seven Years will be required to burn all the weapons.

Ezekiel 39.21 - 29
And I will set My Glory among the nations, and all the nations shall see My Judgment that I Have executed, and my hand that I have laid upon them. And The House of Israel shall know that I am The Lord their God from that Day forward. And the nations shall know that The House of Israel went into exile for their iniquity; because they dealt treacherously against me. Therefore, I Hid My Face from them and Gave them to the hand of their enemies; so they all fell by the sword. According to their uncleanness and according to their transgressions have I done to them, and I Hid My Face from them. Therefore, Thus Says The Lord God: 'Now will I bring back the exile of Jacob, and Have Mercy upon the entire House of Israel, and Will Be Zealous for My Holy Name. They shall forget their shame, and

all their faithlessness in which they have faithless to Me when they dwelt securely in their land, and none made them afraid. After I Have brought them back from the peoples and gathered them out of their enemies' lands, and Am Sanctified in them in the sight of many nations; Then shall they know that I Am The Lord their God, Who Caused them to be led into exile among the nations; but I Have Gathered them to their land and have left there none of them any more. And I Will Not Hide My Face any more from them; for I Have Poured Out My Spirit Upon The House of Israel, Says The Lord God.

The prophecy in Joel 4.10 - 21 bears witness of what is to come. In the Christian Bible see Joel 3.10 - 21. Mystically within the Word יָדִין we Observe a Time of appointment with the Word יָסַד Yaw Sahd meaning Appoint or Set up. That Time of appointment is when The power of the enemies of Israel begins surging with the intent to wipe Israel off the face of the earth and to annihilate all The People of Israel, God Forbid!! We see the formations for this surging beginning to take shape today, 5776 From Creation, with Iran and the nations of the world. America is giving money to Iran. What is the purpose for giving money to Iran? The structure and fortification America offered Israel seems to be evaporating!! What is happening here?

יָדִין
Yaw Deen / To Judge - Justice
74 = 50 ן 10 י 4 ד 10 י

יָסַד
Yaw Sahd / Appoint - Set up
74 = 4 ד 60 ס 10 י

עֵד
Ayd / Witness
74 = 4 ד 70 ע

Deuteronomy 32.43
Rejoice, O you nations, with his people; for he will avenge the blood of his servants, and will render vengeance to his adversaries, and will make expiation for the land of his people.

Moses prophesies that the Nations will rejoice with Israel after The Lord Renders Justice to the offending countries. This Justice is representative of the Second Yod. The Second Yud represents the Time The Lord Renders Judgment against the offending nations. The World will עַד witness what The Lord Does to the Nations. And the Nations will join Israel in praising The Lord for His Glorious Works. Moshiach Ben David begins his rule.

The Prophet Isaiah speaks of this time of rejoicing.

Isaiah 2.1 - 5
The Word that Isaiah the son of Amoz saw concerning Judah and Jerusalem. And it will happen in the End of Days, that the mountain of the Temple of The Lord shall be firmly established as the head of the mountains, and shall be exalted above the hills; and all nations shall flow to it. And many peoples shall go and say, 'Come, and let us go up to The Mountain of The Lord, to The Temple of the God of Jacob; and [Moshiach] will Teach us of His

ways, and we will walk in His paths; for from Zion shall The Torah come forth, and The Word of the Lord from Jerusalem.' And [Moshiach] Shall Judge among the nations, and settle arguments of many people. They shall beat their swords into plowshares, and their spears into pruning hooks; nation shall not lift up sword against nation, nor shall they study warfare any more.

Dear Ones, the subjects of Jewish exile and return, destruction and exultation, major war defeat and victory and Moshiach establishing peace throughout the world are difficult to understand. I don't pretend to be an expert on The End of Days. No one is. We see little bits and pieces that seem to make sense at the time then it changes. I have offered my opinion based upon what I see.

I see the war beginning after The Judgment on Rosh HaShanah. The Lord Hides His Face from The People of Israel. War begins. This is at the conclusion of a Shmittah Year. It appears like we, The People of Israel are going to be annihilated. After Yom Kippur The Lord Brings Justice on the enemy nations. Moshiach's kingdom begins ruling from Jerusalem. The Third Holy Temple is Established. The People of Israel that were scattered by The Lord God are now Gathered back to Israel by Him.

Some who are living today may see the Great Hand of The Lord in the events discussed in this chapter. We are close to the Time known as The End of Days.

Jeremiah 9.22 - 23
Thus Says The Lord, 'Let not the wise man glory in his wisdom, nor let the mighty man glory in his might, let not the rich man glory in his riches; But let him who glories glory in this, that he understands and knows Me, that I Am The Lord Who Exercises Lovingkindness, Justice, and Righteousness, in the earth; for in these things I Delight, Says The Lord.'

So even though we may greatly desire to know about The End of Days we should even more so desire to understand and know The Lord.

Devarim Vezot HaBrachah
Deuteronomy 33.1 - 34.12

Chapter Eleven

The Time of אֵשׁ דָּת The Fiery Torah

Dear Reader, Parshat Vezot HaBrachah concludes this year's Torah Cycle that we began with Parshat Bereisheit in Genesis. God Willing, we are preparing to begin another year of studying The Torah. In this Parshat, we examine Moses Blessing of The Fiery Torah, and a few End of Day prophesies as we complete the entire Torah cycle. Our purpose is to try to understand The Blessing of Moses in Deuteronomy 33.2.

It has been enjoyable learning together, and I hope we can continue in one of our Gematria Books in Genesis.

Devarim 33.2

וַיֹּאמַר יְהֹוָה מִסִּינַי בָּא וְזָרַח מִשֵּׂעִיר לָמוֹ הוֹפִיעַ מֵהַר פָּארָן וְאָתָה מֵרִבְבֹת קֹדֶשׁ מִימִינוֹ אשדת [אֵשׁ דָּת] לָמוֹ:

And He, The Lord Came from Sinai Shining forth [like the sun] from Seir to [The people of Israel]. He Appeared [after coming] from Mount Paran with some of The Holy Myriads and from His Right [Hand He Gave] The Fiery Torah to [The People of Israel].

Esau lived in Mount Seir, Genesis 36.8. Ishmael lived in the wilderness of Paran, Genesis 21.21. Our Sages Teach that The Lord God Offered The Torah to all the nations of the world. The nations of the world declined The Torah. The Torah Observances were offered to Esau and then to Ishmael, the descendants of Abraham. Each declined. Then The Torah Observances were offered to the descendants of Jacob who accepted and embraced The Torah without reservation, Zohar Gimmel 192b.

The nations of the world refused The Torah. Israel accepted The Torah. Parshat Vezot HaBrachah begins with Moses Blessing Israel because The Lord God Dwelt among them, The People of Israel accepted The Torah and acknowledged the sovereignty of The Lord

God, Rabbi Nosson Scherman, The Stone Edition The Chumash (Mesorah Publications, Ltd., Brooklyn, N.Y. 1993), p. 1113.

The Word אשדת means slopes. In Deuteronomy 3.17 we read, 'from the summit of the slopes.' In Deuteronomy 4.49 we read, 'beneath the slopes of the Summit. However in Deuteronomy 33.2 אשדת is translated אֵשׁ דָּת 'Fiery Torah'. We are going to review some Scriptures that Mystically connect the dots of Time with Gematria. The Gematria of אשדת meaning from The [Summit of the Mountain] Slopes is 705. It is upon the Mountain Top that The Lord God descended in a fire. The entire mountain was filled with smoke at the Presence of The Lord God. The Mountain Trembled. The People of Israel were frightened! It is from The Top of The Mountain that The Lord God Gave אֵשׁ דָּת The Fiery Torah. It is from The Top of The Mountain that The House of The Lord will be established at The End of Days.

אשדת
[Mountain] Slopes
705 = 400 ת 4 ד 300 שׁ 1 א

הַכַּפֹּרֶת
Hah Cah Poh Reht / The Mercy [Seat]
705 = 400 ת 200 ר 80 פ 20 כ 5 ה

With the Word אשדת, we see The Lord Descending on top of the mountain slopes, i.e. Mount Sinai to Share The Torah with His People. After the Mount Sinai experience, we see The Lord God direct Moses and The People of Israel to construct the Mishkan / Tabernacle of Meeting. Within the Tabernacle is The Holy Place. The Lord God Communicates with Moses and The People of Israel from The Holy Place.

Exodus 25.22 [KJV 25.23]
And there I Will Meet with you, and I will talk with you from above the cover, from between the Two Cherubim which are upon The Ark of the Testimony, of all things that I Will Give you in Commandment to The People of Israel.

Exodus 25.18
And you shall make Two Cherubim of gold, of hammered workmanship, shall you make them, at the two ends of The Mercy Seat.

Exodus 19.17 - 18
And Moses brought forth the people out of the camp to meet with God, and they stood at the lower part of The Mount. And Mount Sinai was altogether in smoke because The Lord Descended upon it in Fire, and its smoke ascended like the smoke of a furnace, and the whole mount trembled greatly.

Exodus 19.20
And The Lord Came Down upon Mount Sinai, on the top of The Mount; and the Lord Called Moses up to the top of The Mount, and Moses went up.

Ezekiel 43.12
This is instruction regarding The House of Torah / The Temple which is upon the top of The Mount. It's entire surrounding boundaries is a Most Holy Area. Behold! It is The House of The Torah / The Temple.

Isaiah 2.1 - 5
The Word that Isaiah the son of Amoz saw concerning Judah and Jerusalem. And it shall

come to pass in End of Days, that The Mountain of The Lord's House shall be established on The Top of The Mountains, and shall be exalted above the hills; and all nations shall flow to it. And many people shall go and say, Come, and let us go up to The Mountain of The Lord, to The House of The God of Jacob; and [Mosiach] Will Teach us [The Lord's] Ways, and we will walk in His Paths; for from Zion shall go forth The Torah, and The Word of The Lord from Jerusalem. And [Mosiach] shall judge among the nations, and shall decide for many people; and they shall beat their swords into plowshares, and their spears into pruning hooks; nation shall not lift up sword against nation, nor shall they learn war any more. O House of Jacob, come, and let us walk in The Light of The Lord.

Dear Reader, we must remember that Vezot HaBrachah begins with a Blessing from Moses. When Moses Says, 'And He, The Lord Came from Sinai Shining forth [like the sun] from Seir to [The people of Israel]...He Appeared at Mount Paran.' These important events have already happened. It is a Blessing that The Lord God Gave The Torah to The People of Israel. We are forever thankful for The Torah. As noted above we Mystically see the Lord God Speaking to The People of Israel from the Slopes of Mt Sinai and from The Mercy Seat in The Holy Place within The Tabernacle of Meeting. This was in the past. Moses is offering a future Blessing! How can this be?

All the nations of the world rejected The Torah. Many nations in our age reject The Torah. This is a problem for them. They will be Judged for rejecting The Torah. How is it that the nations of the world will repent from rejecting The Torah? How is it that the nations of the world will welcome and accept The Torah of The Lord? What will bring about this change?

Jeremiah 2.3
And many people shall go and say, Come, and let us go up to the mountain of the Lord, to the house of the God of Jacob; and he will teach us of his ways, and we will walk in his paths; for

from Zion shall go forth Torah, and the word of the Lord from Jerusalem.

Why will the nations of the world that in past time now desire to go up to The House of The Lord to worship? What will bring about this change?

Michah 4.1 - 2
But at The End of Days it shall come to pass, that the mountain of The House of The Lord shall be established in the top of the mountains, and it shall be exalted above the hills; and people shall flow to it. And many nations shall come, and say, Come, and let us go up to The Mountain of The Lord, and to The House of The God of Jacob; and he will teach us of his ways, and we will walk in his paths; for Torah shall go forth from Zion, and The Word of The Lord from Jerusalem.

Mystically The change has to do with The Fiery Torah, the Almond and the Menorah. Jeremiah speaks of The Lord God renewing His Torah with His people at The End of Days,

'I will put My Torah in their inward parts, and write [The Torah] in their hearts,' Jeremiah 31.30 [KJV 31.31]. I believe this speaks of The Fiery Torah Moses prophesied in Deuteronomy 33.2. Originally The Torah was written on parchment and tablets of stone. At The End of Days The Torah is written on the hearts of The People of Israel. Mystically the Fiery Torah is like the Menorah and the Almond bowls are like the place where The Fire comes forth.

אֵשׁ דָּת
Aish Dawt / 'Firey Torah'.
705 = 400 ת   4 ד   300 שׁ   1 א

דָּת
Dawt / Law / Torah
404 = 400 ת   4 ד

שָׁקֵד
404 = 4 ד   100 ק   300 שׁ
Shaw Kayd / Almond

אֵשׁ
Aish / Fire
301 = 300 שׁ   1 א

מְנוֹרָה
Menorah
301 = 5 ה 200 ר 6 ו 50 נ 40 מ

What is the Menorah? The Menorah is a Rod with Three branches on the right side and Three branches on the left side. Each Branch of The Menorah has an Almond, i.e. The Light / Fire of The Torah.

Exodus 25.33
And Six branches shall come from its sides; Three branches of The lampstand from the one side, and Three branches of the lampstand from the other side; Three bowls made like Almonds, with a bulb and a flower in one branch; and Three bowls made like Almonds in the other branch, with a bulb and a flower; so for the Six Branches that come from the lampstand.

What do The Almonds represent? The place from where the fire of The Torah comes forth. So in The Blessing of Moses we Mystically see the place in Time where The Light of The Torah comes from within each of The People of Israel.

It has been enjoyable learning together, and I hope we can continue in one of our Gematria Books in Genesis. To view Gematria Books in Genesis please go to:

http://www.bnti.us/bjc16.html.

Scriptural Index

Genesis	Page
1.1	120, 179
2.2-3	156, 157
6.5	168
12.2-3	142
21.21	190
36.8	190
49.1	151

Exodus	Page
12.6	84
19.6	95
19.17-18	193
19.20	193
20.9	94
20.8	94
24.16	16
25.18	192, 193
25.22	192

Exodus	Page
25.33	198
32.15-19	17
32.29-35	17, 18

Leviticus	Page
25.20-22	107, 108
25.34	99, 101
25.34	102

Numbers	Page
12.4	30
12.8	31
12.11	30
12.14	32
13.1-3	32, 33
13.4-16	33
13.6-10	52, 53
13.26-27	34

Numbers	Page
13.27	35
13.28-29	34,35
13.30	35
13.31-33	36
14.1	39, 46
14.2	42, 46
14.3	45, 46
14.4	46
14.5-6	47, 48
14.7-9	48
14.10	47, 49
14.11-19	50
14.20-24	50, 51
14.22-23	52
14.25	55, 56
14.29-32	55
28.26	112
33.38-39	60

Numbers	Page
33.39	16
35.1-7	99, 100
35.2-7	101
35.27	99

Deut.	Page
1.3	22, 87, 88
1.1-3	11,12
1.32	47
1.46	57, 130
2.1	130
2.14	56, 57, 58
3.17	191
3.23	25, 26
4.40	88
4.49	191
6.5-6	91
7.6	96

Deut.	Page	Deut.	Page
7.22	76	9.16	79
8.1	71	9.18	63, 64, 65
8.2	77	9.19	78
8.4	77	9.20	78
8.11	71, 72	9.24	76
8.16	77	9.25	80
8.18	75	10.2	80
8.19	72	10.4	71
9.1	72	10.8	78
9.3	72	10.10	68, 69
9.7	72, 73	10.10-11	20, 21
9.9	63	10.13	73
9.10	67, 70, 71	11.1	80
9.11	63	11.2	73
9.11-12	19	11.4	73
9.12	79	11.8	74
9.12-18	18	11.11	76
9.15-19	19, 20		

Deut.	Page	Deut.	Page
11.12	74	21	134
11.13	74	21.10-11	123, 124
11.21	79	21.13	126
12.8	85	21.18-21	132
13.19	85, 88	21.22-23	134
15.1-3	105	21.27	167
15.5	89	23.16	96
15.15	86	24.16	135
15.7	90	26.11	138, 139
16.16	109	27.26	139
18.1	98	28.1	145
18.1-2	98	28.1-8	141
18.1-5	98, 101	29.9	147
18.1-5	112	30.5	158, 159, 161
18.3-5	97	30.1-7	154, 155, 156
18.5	101	31.27-30	175, 176
20.19	97	31.29	173, 174
21.11	123	32	179

Deut.	Page
32.15-26	180
32.27	181
32.29	173
32.36	176
32.43	185
33.2	189, 191
33.2	197
34.7	15

Joshua	Page
4.19	13, 114
5.9-11	114
5.10-11	13
6.20	13, 14
14.6	116
14.6-10	114, 115
22	119
22.1-4	117

Isaiah	Page
2.1-5	186, 187, 193
27.13	153, 154

Jeremiah	Page
2.3	195, 196
9.22-23	188
31.30	197
32.12-18	161, 162
33	161

Ezekiel	Page
38.8	157, 158
39	182
39.21-29	183, 184
43.12	192, 193

Joel	Page
3.10-21	184
4.10-21	184

Michah	Page
4.1-2	196

Psalms	Page
6.9-10	66
19.10	179
30.6	66
90.4	64
119.71	66, 67
119.89	146
139.12	64
145	143, 144

Ecc.	Page
3.1	11

Gematria Index

Gematria	Page	Gematria	Page
40 – מ	09	111	61
11	12, 13	135	84
18	90	192	149
20 – כ	09	246	14
26	89	248	22
36	179	270	168, 169
38	59	270	171
44	165	301	197, 198
50 – נ	09	318	130
54	91	380	14
59	14	400 ת	57
74	30, 32, 67	404	197
74	83, 143, 185	472	39
74	144, 180	500 ך	09
75	68	700 ן	09
77	118, 119	705	191, 197
80 – פ	09	800 – ף	09
90 – צ	09	90 – ץ	09
104	14	911	119, 120, 121

About The Author

Dr. Akiva Gamliel Belk

Jewish, Husband, Father, Grandfather and Step Great Grandfather.

Graduate:
A.A. Long Beach City College,
B.A. Southern California Bible College,
M.A. Southern California Theological Seminary,
D. Th. Southern California Theological Seminary,
D. Th. Denver Charismatic Theological Seminary

Individual Study:
Rabbi Dovid Nusbaum,
Bais Medrash at Yeshiva Toras Chaim,
Hornosteipler Rebbe, Mordicai Tewerski

Group Study:
Rabbi Yaakov Meyer, Aish Denver
Rabbi Yisroel Engel, Director, Colorado Chabad.

Founder:
Jewishpath.org • Jewishlink.net
• 7Commands.com • Bnti.us

Dean of Jewish Studies
B'nai Noach Torah Institute, LLC

Author of various books.
bnti.us/bjc16.html

Books By Dr. Akiva Gamliel

A Taste Of Gematria Genesis

Gematria Azer is the compilation of each weeks Parshat study for Bereisheit / Genesis for 2013. We dig deep into some subjects like What is The Creator's Revealed Light?, What is it Like to be Perfect? Is Prayer Important?, Who is my SoulMate?, What makes a man the perfect husband? and What are actions of love? There are relevant Gematrias that answer these questions. We discuss and explore them. A brief video based on the center question of each Chapter / Parshat is also available.

A Taste Of Gematria Exodus

We discuss subjects like How do we praise The Lord God? The Lord God Has Chosen the People of Israel to offer praise to Him. Everything that has flesh is to bless His Name. Everyone that has breath is to bless His Name. Each Chapter discusses a different question like: What is the Name of The Lord? What do we really need to know? *You will know that the earth belongs to The Lord... Can one be thankful enough? What is prophecy? Why do we Observe The Commands Of The Lord God... Why should we give?*

A Sincere Journey Ends Without Jesus

This is an autobiography of my spiritual journey. My journey did not begin with the goal of returning to Judaism. My journey began with a desire to give my Baptist Congregation a historical view of Jesus last six days on earth. My journey has been very challenging for me. If you read this book and if you walk in my footprints believing in Jesus will become a challenge for you also. The difference is I am on this side of the journey now. I have returned to Judaism. The journey of my life can be of great help to you if you discern there are problems with the story the New Testament story of Jesus.

Eve Of Creation RESTORED

The Creator Has been so Merciful and Gracious to help me share valuable life restoring Words USING GEMATRIA for Husbands, Wives and family in my new book entitled: Eve Of Creation - RESTORED. The focus of my book is on how to repair and improve oneself and ones relationships. Adam teaches us how to reverse poor choices and improve our lives. Eve Teaches us patience beyond imagination.

Gematria And Mysticism IN GENESIS - BOOK 1

The reader will be introduced to truths not discussed among the religions of the world. Hebrew in the Bible unveils answers to many mysteries. The entire Bible is founded upon Genesis, Exodus, Leviticus, Numbers and Deuteronomy and the truths that flow out of these five books is different than the rest of the Bible. Why? There is a system of Hebrew Letters with which each have a numerical value that have the power to reveal interesting and mystifying relationships within the Hebrew Letters, Words, Phrases etc. of the First Five Books. The cost of this book is a small investment for what the reader will learn.

Gematria And Mysticism IN GENESIS - BOOK II

Book 2 continues where Book 1 concluded. Book 2 covers Genesis Chapters 11 through 20.

Gematria And Mysticism IN GENESIS - BOOK III

Book 3 continues where Book 2 concluded. Book 3

covers Genesis Chapters 21 through 30.

God's Plan From The Beginning
We know that The Lord God Has a plan. We may not know how we fit into His Plan but we do. We discuss sin, salvation, death hell, eternal life, life after death and many more interesting issues.

Mysterious SIGNS Of The Torah in GENESIS
Mysterious SIGNS Of The Torah Revealed In GENESIS is an exploration of Biblical truths organized into the Weekly Parshat study of the Bible. Dr. Akiva Gamliel has been recording and referencing decades of study and research. He has gathered, compiled and organized years of discovery into this mystical book for us to learn, enjoy and share. Many years can pass between one discovery to another which forms a bridge between two discoveries. Revelations are the product of many bridges. Enclosed in this book are some of these special relationships.

Mysterious SIGNS Of The Torah in EXODUS
This is the second in a series of Five Books, God Willing. This book is deep, intense, inspiring and

extremely interesting. Yet, it is easy to read and follow. Dr. Akiva Gamliel includes a Gematria Chart in the beginning of the book . Like each of Dr. Akiva Gamliel's Gematria books there are special Gematrias waiting for the Reader to discover. There is a special sweetness in sharing a Torah Gematria / Sign during a wonderful warm Friday Erev Shabbat meal or another occasion.

Mysterious SIGNS Of The Torah in LEVITICUS
This is the third in a series of Five Books, God Willing. This book is deep, intense, inspiring and extremely interesting. Yet, it is easy to read and follow.

Would You Like To Be Jewish ?
Many readers would like to know what it is like to be Jewish. Some have tried to learn what it is like to be Jewish. Some visited with a Rabbi who may have said, something like this, 'Why do you want to convert? Why do you want to be Jewish? We don't do conversions in Judaism.' You ended up walking away disappointed, angered, exasperated, annoyed and very dissatisfied. This book answers questions about what Jews believe in a way you will not

forget.

Would You Like To Be Jewish 2 ?
This is a continuation of the first book, Would You Like To Be Jewish. In this book we learn that God has always had a plan, even before the beginning of Creation. We learn how God Teaches us to repent when we fail and when we make mistakes. We discover God is very understanding, compassionate and forgiving. We share about fallen angels, Satan, hell and how to live eternally with God.

PASSOVER –
The Last Six Days of Jesus Life On Earth
The Gospel Writers each offer a different perspective of Jesus last six days on Earth. They differ some. I offer my own perspective as a Jew that has been on both sides of this discussion. If you are a Christian... If you believe in Jesus this book will be very challenging. I started on this Journey almost 30 years ago with a desire to give my Baptist Congregation a historical view of Jesus last six days on earth. Since then I have returned to Judaism. I share some of the untold stories and fill in some of the blank pages... My journey can be of great help

to you if you discern there are problems with the story the story the Christian Writers tell of Jesus last six days on earth.

Order Additional Books At:

http://www.bnti.us/books.html

www.ingramcontent.com/pod-product-compliance
Lightning Source LLC
Chambersburg PA
CBHW071703090426
42738CB00009B/1644